P9-BIR-167

LOVING FOOD

A selection of recipes for all occasions

Photography by

Jerry Simpson

BY SARA JANE KASPERZAK

Truly a work of love...all profits from LOVING FOOD will go to the Ronald Michael Kasperzak Kidney Research and Education Fellowship at the Cleveland Clinic in Cleveland, Ohio.

Kathleen Connell, *project manager*

Pamela Hoch, *graphic design*

Sarah Kahle, *recipe tester*

Rick Ellis, *food stylist*

Randy Plimpton, *photography assistant*

Hannah Milman, *prop stylist*

William Smith, *food stylist assistant*

HM Graphics, Inc., *lithography*

Grateful acknowledgement is made to the following for permission to reprint previously published material:

From THE WOLFGANG PUCK COOKBOOK by Wolfgang Puck
Copyright © 1986 Wolfgang Puck
Published by Random House, Inc.

From PACIFIC FLAVORS by Hugh Carpenter and Teri Sandison
Copyright © 1988 Hugh Carpenter
Published by Stewart, Tabori & Chang, Inc., New York

From CHOPSTIX by Hugh Carpenter and Teri Sandison
Copyright © 1990 Hugh Carpenter
Published by Stewart, Tabori & Chang, Inc., New York

From MICHAEL'S COOKBOOK by Michael McCarty
Copyright © 1989 Michael McCarty
Published by Macmillan Publishing Company

From THE ART OF COOKING, VOLUME 2 by Jacques Pepin
Copyright © 1988/1989 Jacques Pepin
Published by Alfred A. Knopf, Inc., New York

From THE HOME CHEF by Judith Ets-Hokin
Copyright © 1988 Judith Ets-Hokin
Published by Celestial Arts

Library of Congress
Cataloging-in-Publication Data

Kasperzak, Sara Jane
LOVING FOOD
A collection of recipes for all occasions

Includes index
1. Cookery I. Title
91-092176 1991
ISBN 0-9630254-0-6

Published by
Commercial Aluminum Cookware Company
P.O. Box 583 Toledo, Ohio 43693

Printed in USA by HM Graphics, Inc.,
Milwaukee, Wisconsin

First Edition

LOVING FOOD is dedicated to Ronald M. Kasperzak,
who gave us Calphalon and changed forever our feelings about cookware.
Ronald loved food and dining. He carefully planned everything from the guest list to the dessert. Ron was totally comfortable in a dining situation. He was challenging, inquiring, relaxed and always enjoyed. Jeff Cooley, friend and associate, said "Ron's approach to dining reflected his life and work. In all things, he displayed the same attention to detail, and respect for the process, and devotion to quality."

INTRODUCTION

My husband, Ronald Kasperzak, is the perfect person to inspire a cookbook, since he wholeheartedly believed that, above all, cooking and entertaining should be fun. He strongly denied any mystique about cooking, and detested cookbooks and articles that intimidated people by listing the potential mistakes in a recipe. Where some might fear tackling a soufflé, he found it the easiest way to interest our children in eating vegetables such as broccoli.

My own involvement with cooking began when I met Ron. Up until that time I had been busy attending law school and then establishing a career, activities that left little time to develop cooking skills. But with Ron's guidance and encouragement, I soon learned that everyone can cook...all it takes is time, patience, and good ingredients.

One important thing he taught me is that most failures still taste good. I remember preparing Turban of Sole for some business friends from out of town. As I turned it out of the pan, it totally collapsed. With a hearty laugh and a good wine, I served it anyway. Our guests still remember the wonderful evening.

Ron enjoyed cooking. His favorite dish to make was liver and onions, a recipe taught to him by a French chef. First, he sautéed perfectly chopped scallions in butter, then set them aside. Next, he placed thinly sliced calf's liver in a very hot pan and sautéed it in butter and olive oil - just 60 seconds on each side. When done, he arranged the sautéed scallions on top and served it immediately. Even I learned to enjoy liver cooked this way.

When we first decided to honor Ron's memory with a cookbook, we wanted to include a wide variety of recipes. We were overwhelmed by the response we received from Ron's many friends, business associates, and famous chefs. We regret that we couldn't use every recipe, but we carefully chose those that we felt you would most enjoy. The result is LOVING FOOD.

Each recipe has been tested in our kitchen and written in an easy-to-follow format. Although the recipes vary in difficulty, even the most elaborate takes only a little more time and patience to prepare. The cookbook features easy-to-read type, since many people (including myself) prefer cooking without their glasses. For quick reference, all recipes are listed under the table ofcontents.

We have listed Calphalon pans when individuals specified using Calphalon, or when they were written in the Calphalon test kitchen. We hope you enjoy trying the recipes in the cookware you have and love.

SARA JANE KASPERZAK

TABLE OF CONTENTS

APPETIZERS & FIRST COURSE DISHES

SOUPS

SALADS

MAIN COURSES

Fish and Shellfish

Beef and Veal

Lamb

Pork

Poultry

Game

PASTA, RICE & RISOTTO

VEGETABLE DISHES

BRUNCH & BREADS

DESSERTS & PASTRIES

Cakes

Cookies and Bars

Pies and Tarts

Desserts

ACKNOWLEDGEMENTS & INDEX

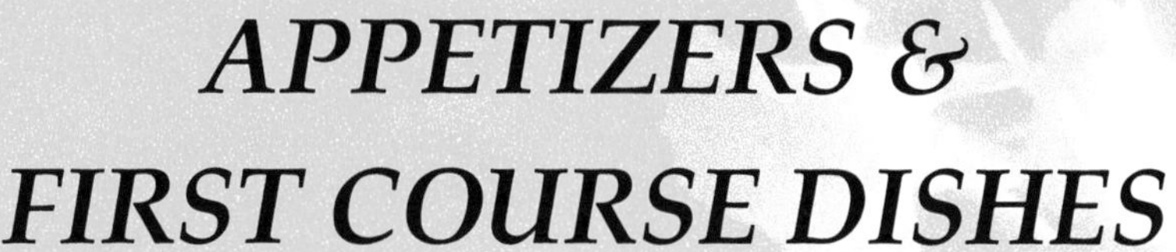

APPETIZERS & FIRST COURSE DISHES

ARTICHOKE FRITTERS
WITH BÉARNAISE SAUCE

---

4 cups peanut or corn oil
1 cup flour
1 teaspoon baking powder
1 egg
1 cup milk
1 teaspoon olive oil
salt and pepper
10 canned artichoke hearts, cut in half

Heat peanut oil in a deep pan. Mix flour and baking powder with egg, milk and olive oil. Season with salt and pepper. Dip artichoke hearts in batter and fry in hot oil until golden brown. Drain on paper towels. Place in bowl and serve with Béarnaise Sauce.

BÉARNAISE SAUCE

---

2 tablespoons chopped shallots
¼ tablespoon tarragon vinegar
6 crushed black peppercorns
2 tablespoons white wine
3 egg yolks
¾ pound butter, melted
⅛ teaspoon salt
pinch of cayenne pepper
juice of ½ lemon
1 teaspoon chopped tarragon leaves

In a heavy weight sauce pan, reduce shallots, vinegar and peppercorns until almost dry. Pour in wine and egg yolks and beat mixture to a thick cream consistency over low heat. Continue heating and stir in melted butter very slowly. Add seasonings and lemon juice, strain and then add chopped tarragon. Keep at moderate temperature.

Gordon Sinclair
Gordon's restaurant
Board Member of the American Institute of Wine and Food
Chicago, Illinois

CAVIAR MOLD

Garnish and serve this mold with lemon slices, chopped egg, sour cream dollops and red or yellow caviar.

---

1 envelope gelatin
½ cup water
1 teaspoon lemon juice
3 ounces cream cheese
16 ounces sour cream
1 teaspoon grated onion juice
dash of Tabasco
1 teaspoon garlic salt
1 teaspoon celery salt
1 teaspoon Durkee's dressing
1 teaspoon mayonnaise
1 cup caviar (2 jars)

Prepare 6 cup mold by greasing with oil, set aside. Dissolve gelatin in water and lemon juice in 2½ quart sauce pan over low heat. Remove from heat and add cream cheese, stir until smooth. Add rest of ingredients, except caviar, to dissolved gelatin mixture and mix well. Fold in caviar carefully, so as not to break. Put mixture into greased mold and chill until firm. To unmold, quickly dip pan in hot water before turning over.

Georgia Welles
Perrysburg, Ohio

FARFALLE WITH SAUSAGE & CREAM

½ pound hot Italian sausage, casings removed
½ pound sweet Italian sausage, casings removed
4 tablespoons butter
1 large clove garlic, minced
½ chicken bouillon cube
½ cup white wine
1 cup heavy cream
¾ tablespoon salt
12 ounces farfalle (bow tie pasta)
½ cup frozen tiny peas

---

serves 8

Brown sausage meat over medium high heat in sauté pan, breaking up large pieces. Remove from pan and drain sausage well on paper towels. Discard any remaining fat in pan. Using same pan, melt butter and sauté garlic until soft. Stir in bouillon and white wine, reduce by half. Pour in heavy cream and simmer on low heat for 5 minutes.

Bring 3 quarts water to boil with ¾ tablespoon salt. Cook farfalle about 12 minutes, stirring occasionally. Drain pasta, stir into sauce, mixing well. Add frozen peas and heat pasta to serving temperature. Serve with grated Parmesan cheese and hot pepper flakes if desired.

Lois Ringelheim
Lois Ringelheim catering
Fairfield, Connecticut

INVOLTINI DI PESCE SPADE E GAMBERI

Fresh Shrimp Wrapped with Swordfish

This recipe can be served as an appetizer, first course, or increase the quantity and serve as an entree with French bread and a green salad.

---

9 ounces swordfish
12 medium scampi/shrimp
3 pieces of shallots
juice of 1 lemon
1 bunch thyme, chopped
1 cup vermouth
1 tablespoon chopped green bell pepper
$1/2$ cup sweet butter
1 tomato, chopped

---

serves 4

Cut the swordfish into 12 thin slices. Shell and devein shrimp, wrap a swordfish slice around each piece, put wrapped pieces in bowl. Mix one chopped shallot, lemon juice, thyme and a pinch of salt and pour over wrapped shrimp. Marinate for 30 minutes.

Chop 2 remaining shallots and sauté in pan. Pour in vermouth and green pepper, simmer for 3 minutes on low heat. Whisk in butter a little at a time until mixture is creamy.

Sauté swordfish wrapped shrimp on a griddle for 3 minutes. Serve with the butter sauce and chopped tomatoes on top.

Piero Selvaggio
Valentino's restaurant
Santa Monica, California

MARCO POLO DUMPLINGS
WITH CHINESE SALAD DRESSING

Hugh Carpenter named these dumplings after the famous Italian explorer to the Far East. The act of tossing is the Italian part, the dumplings and salad dressing are authentic Chinese. Serve as an appetizer or entree.

---

4 dried black Chinese mushrooms
6 water chestnuts, preferably fresh
2 green onions
1 pound raw shrimp
1 egg white
1 tablespoon cornstarch
1 tablespoon light soy sauce
2 teaspoons dry sherry
1 teaspoon Oriental sesame oil
½ teaspoon Chinese chili sauce
¼ teaspoon salt
30 won ton skins
cornstarch for dusting
Chinese Salad Dressing
2 tablespoons white sesame seeds

---

serves 6-8

To prepare filling, soak mushrooms in hot water until soft, about 20 minutes. Cut off and discard stems. Peel fresh water chestnuts, if using. Cut green onions into small pieces. Mince mushroom caps, water chestnuts and green onions together by hand or in a food processor.

Shell and devein shrimp. Coarsely chop shrimp along with the egg white by hand or in a food processor. Do not mince so finely that its texture is destroyed. Combine shrimp with mushroom mixture and add 1 tablespoon cornstarch, soy sauce, sherry, sesame oil, chili sauce and salt. Mix thoroughly.

Trim won tons into circles. Place 2 teaspoons of filling in the center of each won ton. Moisten the edges with water and fold dumplings in half over filling, being careful not to flatten filling. Press edges together. Dumplings will be half-moon shaped. Moisten each end of dumpling, then touch the moistened ends together. The dumplings should look like little caps. Place on a layer of waxed paper lightly dusted with cornstarch. Refrigerate, uncovered until ready to cook, but no more than 5 hours.

Make Chinese Salad Dressing. In a small ungreased skillet set over high heat, stir sesame seeds until light golden. Immediately pour out and set aside.

Bring 4 quarts of water to a vigorous boil. Add the dumplings and give them a gentle stir. When the dumplings float to the surface, about 3 minutes, gently tip into a colander to drain.

Transfer dumplings to a mixing bowl and toss with dressing. Remove dumplings to a heated serving platter and sprinkle with toasted sesame seeds. Serve at once.

CHINESE SALAD DRESSING

---

2 tablespoons light soy sauce
2 tablespoons dry sherry
¼ cup red wine vinegar
2 tablespoons Oriental sesame oil
2 teaspoons hoisin sauce
2 teaspoons sugar
1 teaspoon Chinese chili sauce
2 cloves garlic, finely minced
1 tablespoon finely minced fresh ginger
1 tablespoon grated or finely minced tangerine or orange peel
3 tablespoons finely minced fresh coriander (cilantro)
4 tablespoons finely minced green onions

Combine all dressing ingredients. Puree in food processor, then transfer to a small dish.

HUGH CARPENTER
Chopstix restaurants
Author of CHOPSTIX and PACIFIC FLAVORS cookbooks
Member of the International Association of Culinary Professionals
Los Angeles, California

MELROSE AVENUE SPRING ROLLS

These spring rolls have an unusual, spicy flavor if you use the Mexican or Portuguese sausage called chorizo, or substitute a spicy American or Italian sausage.

Hugh Carpenter advises buying 6 inch square or round sheets called spring roll skins from Asian markets and avoid using American egg roll wrappers. Spring roll skins are sold frozen and can be thawed and refrozen many times.

1/2 pound chorizo or other spicy sausage
1 ounce rice sticks
6 dried Chinese black mushrooms
2 cups shredded green cabbage
2 cups bean sprouts
1 cup julienned carrots
2 green onions, minced
2 tablespoons dry sherry
1 tablespoon oyster sauce
1 tablespoon Oriental sesame oil
1 teaspoon Chinese chili sauce
1/2 teaspoon sugar
3 cloves garlic, finely minced
2 tablespoons cornstarch
3 cups plus 2 tablespoons cooking oil
12 to 14 spring roll skins
2 eggs, well beaten
dipping sauces
20 bibb lettuce leaves

---

serves 8-12

If the sausage is in links, slit the casing and squeeze the meat out. Place the sausage meat in a small frying pan or stir fry. Cook over low heat until thoroughly cooked and the fat is rendered, about 15 minutes. Stir occasionally. Transfer to a sieve and press the meat with the back of a spoon to eliminate all fat. If the sausage meat is still in lumps, chop finely.

Soak the rice sticks in hot water for 20 minutes. Drain and cut into 2 inch lengths. Soak the mushrooms in hot water until soft, about 20 minutes. Discard the stems and shred the caps.

Combine the sausage, mushrooms, rice sticks, cabbage, bean sprouts, carrots and green onions. Separately, combine the sherry, oyster sauce, sesame oil, chili sauce, sugar and garlic. Combine the cornstarch with an equal amount of cold water and set aside.

Place a 12 inch skillet or wok over high heat. When hot, add 2 tablespoons cooking oil. When the oil becomes hot, add the sausage mixture. Stir fry until the vegetables are brightly colored, about 2 minutes, then add the sauce. Stir fry until the vegetables just begin to wilt, about 1 minute more. Add a little of the cornstarch mixture to thicken the sauce, then transfer to a bowl. Cool to room temperature, and then place in freezer until thoroughly chilled, about 1 hour.

Separate the spring roll skins. Position each spring roll so one of the corners is pointing at you. Place about 1/2 cup of the filling in the bottom third of the skin and then form the filling into a cylinder, stretching between the side corners. Bring the corner nearest you over the center of the filling and then tuck the tip under the filling. Roll the spring roll a turn. Brush all the edges and along the top of the cylinder with beaten egg. Bring the two side corners one-third over the top of the cylinder. Now finish rolling the spring roll into a cylinder. Place on a small tray as you complete the rest of the spring rolls. Store, unstacked and uncovered, in the refrigerator up to one day ahead.

When ready to serve, place 3 cups of oil in a 12 inch skillet and heat over high heat. When the oil reaches 370 degrees (bubbles will escape from the end of a wooden spoon when placed into the oil for 10 seconds), fry the spring rolls in 3 batches, cooking them on both sides until light golden, about 3 minutes. Drain on a wire rack.

Heat the oil again, this time until it reaches 400 degrees. Fry the spring rolls a second time in 2 batches until they are dark golden, about 1 minute. Drain. The second frying makes the spring rolls crispier.

Serve spring rolls whole or cut in half with one or more dipping sauces. Guests should wrap a spring roll in a lettuce leaf, dip in sauce and enjoy.

HUGH CARPENTER
Chopstix restaurants
Author of CHOPSTIX and PACIFIC FLAVORS cookbooks
Member of the International Association of Culinary Specialists
Los Angeles, California

PERESTROIKA PIZZA

This recipe was created and prepared for a Cancer Center fund raising event at the University of California at San Diego. Create a different version of the appetizer each time you make this by varying the suggested crusts.

---

10 ounce refrigerated pizza crust dough, or
premade pizza crust, large pita bread, or several tortillas
12 ounces Brie cheese
8 ounces smoked salmon, thinly sliced
2 ounces golden, pink or red caviar
fresh dill or fennel for garnish

---

serves 12

Preheat oven to 425 degrees.

If using a refrigerated pizza crust dough, follow package directions. If using premade crust, pita bread or tortillas, use enough to provide about 36 square inches of surface.

Bake refrigerated dough for approximately 5 minutes. After baking, turn oven to 475 degrees. Premade crust, pita bread and tortillas should remain at room temperature.

Top the crust with ¼ inch slices of Brie cheese. Bake 5 minutes, then cool to room temperature.

Cover with a thin layer of smoked salmon. Garnish with caviar and fresh dill or fennel. Cut into 12 individual portions, either wedge shaped or oblong depending on crust shape.

George Gruenwald
New Product Development Group
Board Member of the American Institute of Wine and Food
Rancho Santa Fe, California

PIZZA FONDUE

A great hors d'oeuvre for a teenage gathering or a Sunday afternoon television sporting event.

---

1 pound ground beef
1 small onion, chopped
1 tablespoon butter or margarine
1/4 teaspoon garlic powder
1/4 teaspoon oregano
1 tablespoon cornstarch
20 ounces pizza sauce
8 ounces shredded mozzarella cheese
10 ounces shredded cheddar cheese

---

serves 6

Brown beef and onion in butter. Add dry ingredients to beef mixture, then stir in pizza sauce. Add 1/3 of the cheese at a time until melted. Pour into a fondue pot and serve with French bread cut into cubes.

KEITH AND DIANE HEINER
Rolling Pin
Plantation, Florida

PIZZETTAS

Use other varieties of cheese for this simple and delicious appetizer. Pizzettas are very good served with a glass of Robert Mondavi Fume Blanc.

¼ cup olive oil with 2 cloves garlic, chopped
24 slices of thinly sliced baguette French bread
24 slices of tomatoes, approximately same size as bread
1 tablespoon fresh minced parsley
1 tablespoon fresh minced basil
24 slices of fontina or Gruyère cheese, approximately same size as bread
freshly ground pepper

---

yields 24

Using pastry brush, brush each bread slice with garlic fragrant olive oil. In very hot oven, broiler or salamander, toast top of bread slices to golden brown.

Layer slice of tomato on bread, sprinkle with parsley and basil. Top with cheese slice and put under the broiler or very hot oven until cheese is melted. Just before serving, sprinkle with freshly ground pepper.

MARGRIT AND BOB MONDAVI
Robert Mondavi Winery, Oakville, California
Honorary Chairman of the Board of Directors of the American Institute of Wine and Food

PUMPKIN CARRIAGES

An easy, colorful, first course for autumn dinners. If the squash skin is tender, it is edible.

---

4 to 5 miniature pumpkins (about 8 ounces each)
10 ounces herb Boursin cheese
2 egg yolks and 1 egg white
thyme sprigs
black pepper

---

serves 4-5

Pierce pumpkins with a metal skewer in one place only. Steam in a covered steamer over simmering water until squash are tender when pierced with the skewer.

Let cool, then slice off top of each squash making the top a lid. Scoop out and discard seeds and coarse fibers leaving shell and flesh intact.

Blend cheese and eggs, season with pepper. Spoon equally into each squash, using all of the mixture, which can mound slightly. Chill covered up to 4 hours if done ahead.

Steam filled squash in steamer over boiling water until filling is set in center, about 15 minutes. Add squash lids to steamer the last 5 minutes to warm. Lay thyme sprigs on cheese, set lids in place and serve hot.

Jerry DiVecchio
Food and Entertaining Editor, SUNSET magazine
Board Member of the American Institute of Wine and Food
Menlo Park, California

SAUSAGE, APPLE & BLEU CHEESE BOUCHÉE

1 pound fresh sage sausage
1 medium red onion, chopped
3 cloves garlic, minced
2 McIntosh apples, cored, peeled, grated
4 ounces bleu cheese
1 tablespoon chopped fresh basil
1 teaspoon chopped fresh thyme
2 eggs
salt and pepper
bread crumbs, if needed
Pâte à Choux au Fromage
kosher salt

Brown the sausage in a large sauté pan, breaking it up with a fork to insure small pieces. When the sausage is cooked half way, stir in the chopped onion and garlic. Continue cooking until the sausage is fully cooked and then place in a colander over a large bowl to drain off grease. Drain at least 15 minutes, stirring occasionally to remove excess grease.

Meanwhile, combine grated apples, bleu cheese, fresh basil, fresh thyme and eggs in a large mixing bowl. Add the drained sausage mixture and combine thoroughly. Season with salt and pepper. Add some bread crumbs if too moist. The mixture should hold together.

Preheat oven to 400 degrees.

Make choux pastry. Put the choux pastry in a pastry bag with a medium star tip. On a greased cookie sheet pipe small stars 2 inches apart. Take 1 tablespoon of the sausage mixture, and using your hands, place on top of each star. Form the mixture into a small cone. Take your pastry bag filled with the Pâte à Choux and spiral each sausage cone with the pastry, building the pastry from the bottom to the top about 3 times around. Sprinkle with a touch of kosher salt and cracked pepper. Bake immediately for 17 to 20 minutes. Serve immediately.

PÂTE À CHOUX AU FROMAGE

CHOUX PASTRY WITH CHEESE

3/4 cup water
3 tablespoons unsalted butter
salt
3/4 cup flour
1 ounce grated Parmesan cheese
3 eggs
pepper
Tabasco

Bring water, butter and salt to a boil in a sauce pan. Add flour, stir vigorously until the flour and water form a thick dough. Place in a food processor, add the cheese and process until combined. Add pepper and Tabasco to taste. Add eggs one at a time, until a smooth and shiny dough has formed. Best when used immediately.

MATTHEW WESTON
Matthew's Creative Cuisine restaurant and catering
Toledo, Ohio

SHRIMP IN CREAM CHEESE SAUCE

1 pound fresh shrimp
water or stock
20 ounces cream of shrimp soup
6 ounces cream cheese
8 ounces sliced water chestnuts
1 tablespoon minced parsley
2 teaspoons lemon juice
1/4 teaspoon garlic salt
1/4 teaspoon paprika
1/2 cup sherry

serves 4

Peel and devein shrimp. In a medium sauce pan bring water or stock to boil. Drop the shrimp into the liquid, immediately reduce heat. Simmer for about 3 minutes depending on size. Remove from heat and drain shrimp at once to prevent curling up. Set aside.

Over low heat in a sauce pan, heat soup and cheese until melted. Stir in remaining ingredients, cook until heated through. Serve over rice.

Polly Webb
Toledo, Ohio

SHRIMP & SCALLOP STIR FRY

Chuck Williams developed this recipe for the Williams-Sonoma catalogue. In fact, he said the Calphalon stir fry pan provided the inspiration.

½ pound fresh, medium shrimp
½ pound small bay scallops, or large ones cut in half
salt
water
3 tablespoons vegetable oil
1 cup fresh shelled peas
2 teaspoons cornstarch
1 green onion, sliced into ½ inch pieces
½ red bell pepper, thinly sliced
1 tablespoon dry sherry
2 teaspoons sesame oil (optional)

---

serves 4-6

Shell and devein shrimp and combine with scallops in a bowl together with 1 teaspoon salt and ½ cup water. Let stand for 15 minutes, then rinse several times and pat dry with paper towels. In a bowl, toss shrimp and scallops in 1 tablespoon vegetable oil, reserve. Blanch peas in a pot of boiling water for 1 to 2 minutes, drain, chill in ice water, then drain again and set aside.

Mix cornstarch with 3 tablespoons water and a pinch of salt, set aside.

Heat 2 tablespoons vegetable oil in a stir fry pan, add the shrimp and scallops, stir and toss until shrimp turn pink, about 1 minute. Remove with slotted spoon and reserve. Add green onion and red bell pepper to pan and toss for a few seconds. Return shrimp and scallops to pan. Stir in sherry and cornstarch mixture. Toss quickly for a few seconds until sauce is thickened. Stir in peas. For added flavor and shine, sprinkle sesame oil over shrimp and scallops, and give a quick stir. Serve immediately with steamed rice.

CHUCK WILLIAMS
Williams-Sonoma
San Francisco, California

SPARERIBS
WITH SECRET CHINESE BARBECUE SAUCE

Five-spice powder is a spice blend found in Oriental markets and many supermarkets.

---

3 pounds spareribs
Secret Chinese Barbecue Sauce

---

serves 6-8

Preheat oven to 350 degrees. Line a large baking pan with foil. Coat a wire rack with cooking spray, then place rack in baking pan.

Cut off the flap on meat on underside of ribs. Also on underside is a tough white membrane, using a sharp pointed knife, loosen membrane along the bone at one edge, then gripping membrane with a paper towel, pull it away. Set aside.

Make Secret Chinese Barbecue Sauce. Rub spareribs on both sides with barbecue sauce and place on the rack, meat side up. Bake until meat begins to shrink away from the ends of the bones, about 1 hour.

Cut into individual ribs. Serve hot or at room temperature.

SECRET CHINESE BARBECUE SAUCE

---

5 tablespoons hoisin sauce
3 tablespoons plum sauce
2 tablespoons oyster sauce
2 tablespoons dark soy sauce
2 tablespoons honey
1 tablespoon dry sherry
1 tablespoon peanut oil
1 teaspoon Chinese chili sauce (optional)
½ teaspoon five-spice powder
1 tablespoon finely minced garlic
1 tablespoon finely minced fresh ginger

---

yields 1¼ cups

Combine all ingredients for barbecue sauce.

Hugh Carpenter
Chopstix restaurants
Author of CHOPSTIX and PACIFIC FLAVORS cookbooks
Los Angeles, California

SUMMER MINT PASTA

Japanese chilies (or substitute Chinese dried chilies) are found at some supermarkets and Oriental stores. This dish can be served as a first course or entree.

---

6 large tomatoes
4 Japanese chilies, coarsely chopped
½ cup Italian extra virgin olive oil
4 large cloves garlic, peeled, coarsely chopped
1 purple onion, julienned
1 white onion, julienned
2 ounces fresh mint, chopped very fine
salt and black pepper
1 pound spaghetti

---

serves 4

Process tomatoes in blender, remove seeds, and reserve. Cook chilies in oil, until oil takes on the chilies "hot" flavor, do not brown. Remove chilies and discard. Cook garlic and onions slowly in the "hot" oil until very soft, about 30 minutes, do not brown. Add tomatoes and cook until mixture coats spoon. Season mixture with salt and pepper and then add chopped mint. Cook spaghetti to al dente. Drain. Pour sauce over cooked pasta and toss.

BRUCE MARDER
West Beach Cafe, Rebecca's, DC Three and Broadway Deli restaurants
Venice, California

pictured
potato & zuchini soup, 36
pizzettas, 12
sautéed quail with herb polenta stuffing, 116

1988
Napa Valley
BLANC
Dry Sauvignon Blanc
MONDAVI WINERY

SOUPS

ASPARAGUS SORREL SOUP

Sorrel, a lemon tasting green, is widely used in France. It is wonderful in salads and complements fish. If you are unable to find sorrel, substitute spinach and add a little lemon juice to compensate for the flavor. The soup can be served warm or chilled.

---

2 pounds medium stalk asparagus
2 cups cleaned sorrel leaves
2 tablespoons olive oil
4 to 6 tablespoons butter
1 cup chopped leeks, white parts only, well cleaned
1/4 cup white rice
6 cups chicken stock
salt and pepper
3/4 cup heavy cream

---

serves 6-8

Peel asparagus and chop into 1 inch pieces. Discard tough ends and reserve 8 tips for garnish. Coarsely chop sorrel leaves and reserve 6 to 8 leaves for garnish.

Heat butter and olive oil in heavy 8 quart pan. Sauté leeks, stirring until softened, about 4 to 5 minutes. Add asparagus and sorrel, toss and stir another 3 to 4 minutes.

Pour in chicken stock, rice, and salt and pepper to taste. Simmer and cook until asparagus is tender, about 20 minutes.

Cool slightly and puree in blender or processor. Return to pan and gently whisk in cream, adjust seasonings. Cool and garnish with sautéed asparagus tips, cut in half, and tiny sorrel leaf slivers.

Roger Mandle
Deputy Director of the National Gallery of Art, Washington, D.C.
Former Director of the Toledo Museum of Art, Toledo, Ohio

BORSCHT

After years of trying to perfect this recipe, Ron finally admitted this Borscht recipe was better than the one he ordered regularly at a favorite restaurant. A wonderful first course for summer entertaining. Chill the bowls or soup plates and the Borscht will stay cold until your guests enjoy it.

---

10 cups chicken broth
2 cups uncooked beets, cut into 1 inch long julienne strips
4 cups chopped uncooked beets
1½ cups finely chopped carrots
1½ cups finely chopped onions
½ cup balsamic vinegar or ¾ cup red wine vinegar
salt (optional)
3 egg yolks
3 tablespoons sugar
2 cups sour cream
3 tablespoons freshly squeezed lemon juice
2 cups thinly diced cucumber, with peel
½ cup fresh dill weed, minced

---

serves 10

In an 8 quart stock pot, add 8 cups of chicken broth. Place remaining 2 cups of chicken broth in a sauce pan and add julienned beets. Cover and simmer over medium heat for 8 to 10 minutes, or until beets are tender. Strain, reserving the julienned beets, and add the liquid to the chicken broth in the stock pot.

Bring broth to a boil and add chopped beets, carrots, onions and vinegar. Season to taste with salt. Cover, turn the heat down and simmer for 20 to 25 minutes until vegetables are tender. Strain chicken/beet broth into a large bowl and chill for 3 hours or overnight. Discard vegetables.

Mix together egg yolks, sugar, sour cream and lemon juice, until smooth. Whisk this into the chilled broth, stirring until smooth. Chill until ready to serve.

Prior to serving, place 2 tablespoons of the reserved julienned beets and 2 tablespoons of diced cucumber in each soup bowl. Ladle borscht into bowls and sprinkle with fresh minced dill weed.

SARA JANE KASPERZAK

BOUNDARY WATERS WILD RICE SOUP

This is a favorite using Minnesota wild rice, but you can substitute with another variety. Garnish with either enokitake mushrooms or a slice of lemon. Makes a wonderful first course!

---

4 cups chicken stock
1/4 cup chopped onion
1 tablespoon butter
2 to 3 tablespoons flour
3/4 to 1 cup cooked Minnesota wild rice
1/2 teaspoon white pepper
1 cup whipping cream
1/3 cup sherry

---

yields 6 cups

Heat stock in a small sauce pan. In a large sauce pan, sauté onion in butter until tender. Stir flour into butter mixture making a roux, stir over heat 2 to 3 minutes. Slowly add heated stock to roux, whisking until smooth. Heat to boiling, reduce heat and simmer 20 minutes. To make thicker, add more roux. Add wild rice, pepper and cream, simmer 5 to 10 minutes. Add sherry and heat thoroughly.

MINNESOTA WILD RICE

---

1 cup uncooked Minnesota wild rice
3 cups water, bouillon or broth
1/2 teaspoon salt

---

yields 3 cups

In large sauce pan, combine wild rice, water and salt, heat to boiling. Reduce heat, cover, and simmer about 30 minutes. Check for doneness. Continue simmering until tender, checking every 5 minutes. Wild rice usually cooks tender in 30 to 45 minutes. Cooked wild rice can be stored in a tightly covered container up to 2 weeks in the refrigerator or freeze for longer storage.

Courtesy of JIM STIRRATT, GEORGE COLLINS, KAREN DODGE
Dayton's Marshall Field's Hudson's
Minneapolis, Minnesota

CALIFORNIA CULINARY ACADEMY FISH SOUP

---

2 to 3 pounds fish filets
6 tablespoons margarine
6 onions, sliced
1 clove garlic, chopped
8 cups water
6 medium size potatoes, peeled, quartered
2 bay leaves
½ teaspoon marjoram
⅓ cup chopped parsley
½ teaspoon thyme
½ teaspoon salt
½ teaspoon pepper

---

serves 8-10

Cut fish into bite size pieces, reserve. Melt margarine in stock pot and sauté onion and garlic until translucent. Add water, potatoes and seasonings. Cover and cook potatoes until tender. To the gently boiling broth, add fish and continue cooking for 10 to 15 minutes, stirring once very gently, until the fish flakes easily.

Brother H. Zaccarelli
California Culinary Academy
San Francisco, California

CRAB BISQUE

Crab Bisque is a favorite Northwest dish. This recipe can easily be doubled or tripled for large groups.

---

2 pounds crabmeat
2 tablespoons Worcestershire sauce
1 cup dry vermouth
2 tablespoons unsalted butter
2 carrots, shredded
1 onion, diced
46 ounces clear chicken broth
$10\frac{1}{2}$ ounces tomato soup
1 quart whipping cream
salt and pepper

---

serves 8

Mix Worcestershire sauce and dry vermouth, pour over crabmeat. Let marinate for 30 minutes before adding to soup.

Sauté carrots and onion in butter in an 8 quart stock pot. Pour in chicken broth, tomato soup, crab mixture and whipping cream. Season with salt and pepper. Simmer for 1 to 2 hours.

RUTHANN PANOWICZ
Drees
Olympia, Washington

CREAM OF BROCCOLI SOUP

1 small bunch broccoli (3½ cups)
1½ cups water
½ teaspoon salt
1¾ cups clear chicken broth
2½ cups milk
½ pound American cheese, cut in cubes
3 tablespoons margarine
4 tablespoons cornstarch
½ cup sour cream

serves 6

Chop broccoli very fine. Boil broccoli in covered sauce pan in 1 cup water plus salt for 5 minutes. Do not drain. Add chicken broth, milk, cheese and margarine. Heat thoroughly over medium heat, stirring frequently. Do not boil. Mix cornstarch and ½ cup water. Stir until thin. Add to soup, stirring frequently until thickened. Separately, combine sour cream and ½ cup of hot mixture, stirring until well blended. Return mixture to soup and stir until thoroughly heated and blended.

Jan Deckard
Rolling Pin
Jacksonville, Florida

CREAM OF CILANTRO & YUCCA ROOT SOUP

Part of a Southwest Cooking Seminar, this is an alternative to traditional vichyssoise.

---

2 tablespoons butter
1 cup chopped white onion
5 cups chicken stock
10 ounces yucca root, peeled, cut in ½ inch slices
5 tablespoons chopped fresh cilantro
½ cup heavy cream
⅛ teaspoon black pepper
⅛ teaspoon red pepper
salt

---

serves 6

Preheat a Calphalon 4½ quart sauce pan on medium heat, then add butter. When butter is bubbling, sauté onions 3 to 4 minutes. Stir in chicken stock, yucca root and cilantro, bring to a boil. When stock starts to boil, reduce heat and maintain a soft boil for 20 minutes. Puree soup in food processor to a fine consistency. Strain mixture through a fine mesh strainer or chinois to remove any lumps. Return to heat, enrich with cream, season with salt and pepper. Serve warm or chilled. Garnish wih a fresh cilantro leaf.

Paul Angelo LoGiudice
Culinary Events Specialist
Commercial Aluminum Cookware Company

CREAM OF SORREL SOUP

Fresh sorrel can be substituted for processed sorrel. If fresh is used, simply blanch in salted, boiling water and puree with chicken broth. If you are unable to find sorrel leaves, substitute spinach leaves and add a little lemon juice.

---

1 cup butter
2 cups potatoes, peeled, diced
1 medium onion, minced
½ cup diced carrots
1 cup diced celery
2 bay leaves
½ cup chopped parsley
white pepper
garlic powder
2 quarts well seasoned chicken stock
¼ cup flour
¼ cup cornstarch
2 cups half and half
1 quart sour cream
13 ounces sorrel, packed in water

Melt butter in heavy sauce pot. Add the potatoes, onion, carrots, celery and sauté until they start to soften, do not brown. Add bay leaves, parsley, and seasonings to taste. Pour in chicken stock and continue to cook until potatoes are tender.

Create a slurry by blending flour, cornstarch, and half and half. Using a wire whisk, stir into soup. Once soup returns to a boil, remove from heat.

Stir together sour cream and sorrel. Blend some of the hot soup into the sorrel mixture to warm, then combine with rest of soup.

Carolyn Buster
The Cottage restaurant
Member of the International Associaton of Culinary Professionals
Calumet City, Illinois

CRUNCHY GAZPACHO SOUP

This gazpacho has a mild flavor making it a soup the whole family can enjoy. For a spicier version substitute V-8 juice for tomato juice, and season with Tabasco and additional cumin.

---

1 clove garlic
1 medium onion
½ cup green bell pepper
½ cup cucumber
3 pounds tomatoes (5 medium to large), peeled
2 cups tomato juice
½ teaspoon cumin
1 tablespoon salt
¼ cup olive oil
¼ cup wine vinegar
black pepper

---

serves 6

Chop garlic first, then onion, green pepper, cucumber and tomatoes in food processor. Be careful not to over process, vegetables should remain crunchy. Combine chopped vegetables with rest of ingredients in bowl, pepper to taste. Chill at least 3 hours so flavors will marry.

Anne and Bob Oswald
Indianapolis, Indiana

GUMBO FILÉ

Indians along the legendary Singing River in Mississippi discovered that ground sassafras leaves (filé powder) would thicken and flavor food. Used in this gumbo recipe, filé heightens the wonderful flavors of oysters, crab and shrimp. It's a hearty soup with wonderful flavors in every bite!

3/4 pound shelled raw shrimp
1 pint oysters and liquid
1/2 pound crabmeat
1/2 cup butter
2 tablespoons flour
1 onion, finely chopped
1 pound okra, cut in bite size pieces
2 quarts hot water
1 cup chopped tomatoes
2 tablespoons chopped celery leaves
2 tablespoons chopped green bell pepper
2 small cloves garlic, chopped
1 tablespoon gumbo filé powder

---

serves 10

In 8 quart stock pot over low flame, while stirring constantly, blend butter and flour until it begins to take on color. Then add onions and sauté until slightly brown. Add the cut okra and continue stirring until the moisture has evaporated. When okra is browned, pour in hot water and oyster liquid, mixing well. Stir in tomatoes, celery leaves, green pepper, garlic and crabmeat. Simmer for 30 minutes. Add shrimp, oysters and filé powder, cook for an additional 30 minutes. Serve in hot soup plates over rice.

Pat Stanley
Aropi, Inc.
Atlanta, Georgia

POTATO & ZUCCHINI SOUP

---

2 tablespoons butter
1½ cups sliced leeks
4 cups chicken stock
1 pound potatoes, cubed
2 tablespoons chopped parsley
½ teaspoon salt
2 zucchinis, cubed
pepper
½ cup heavy cream

---

serves 4

Preheat a Calphalon 4½ quart sauce pan on medium heat. Heat butter, then sauté leeks 5 to 8 minutes. Add chicken stock, potatoes, parsley and salt. Bring to a boil, reduce heat, cover and allow to simmer for 10 minutes.

Stir in zucchini and continue simmering for another 10 minutes. Puree soup in a food processor. Return to pan and add pepper to taste. Enrich with cream. Serve warm or chilled.

Paul Angelo LoGiudice
Culinary Events Specialist
Commercial Aluminum Cookware Company

PUMPKIN BLACK BEAN SOUP

Glen serves this soup as a first course for Christmas dinner with the Roast Pork Loin Stuffed with Fruit. The combination of different flavors complement each other well.

---

1 pound black beans
2 tablespoons butter
2 large onions, minced
1 celery rib, minced
2½ quarts water
1 bay leaf
6 whole cloves
12 peppercorns
3 cups pumpkin puree
2 teaspoons salt
sour cream
chopped onion
chopped parsley

---

serves 8

Soak black beans overnight, drain. Sauté minced onion and celery in butter in 8 quart Calphalon stock pot. When onions are translucent, add black beans along with water and bouquet garni (bay leaf, cloves and peppercorns tied up in cheesecloth). Bring to a boil, then let simmer slowly for 2½ hours, stirring occasionally. Add up to ½ quart more water, if necessary. Add pumpkin puree and salt, cook another 30 minutes or until beans are falling apart. Season to taste. Serve garnished with a dollop of sour cream and a heaping tablespoon of chopped onion and parsley.

GLEN SENK
Williams-Sonoma
San Francisco, California

SALMON SOUP

2 pounds salmon filets
6 tablespoons butter
4 small onions, minced
4 cloves garlic, minced
1 pound potatoes, skins on, chopped in ½ inch pieces
1 bay leaf
2 grams saffron
dash of cayenne
dash of salt and pepper
8 cups fish stock
2 cups cream
1 tablespoon cognac
½ cup minced parsley
1 cup croutons
¼ cup grated Parmesan cheese

serves 8-10

Prepare fish stock. Cut salmon into bite size pieces. Melt butter, sauté onions and garlic 4 to 5 minutes. Stir in potatoes, cook 2 to 3 minutes. Add seasonings to taste and pour in fish stock. Simmer 15 to 20 minutes until potatoes are almost tender. Stir in salmon and cook 3 to 4 minutes. Pour in cream and cognac and adjust seasonings. Garnish with parsley, croutons and cheese.

FISH STOCK

5 pounds fish bones
2 onions, chopped
3 stalks celery, chopped
2 carrots, chopped
2 bay leaves
1 handful parsley
3½ quarts water
2 cups white wine

yields 8 cups

Place all ingredients in 8 quart stock pot. Bring to a boil, reduce heat, then simmer for 30 minutes. Strain broth. An alternative method for added flavor is to brown bones and vegetables in a 350 degree oven in an uncovered roasting pan for 15 to 20 minutes. Then place in pot with water and wine, bring to boil, simmer for 30 minutes. Strain broth.

CAROLYN YORSTON
Board Member of the American Institute of Wine and Food
La Jolla, California

SALADS

BULGARIAN SALAD
OF ROASTED PEPPERS, ROASTED ONIONS AND WALNUTS

6 medium red onions, rubbed with olive oil
6 large red bell peppers
3 cups walnuts
12 small handfuls of arugula
2 cups feta cheese, crumbled (optional)
Garlic Vinaigrette

serves 12

Preheat oven to 400 degrees. Place onions in a baking pan, and roast until tender but not mushy. This may take as long as an hour. When the onions are cool enough to handle, remove skin and cut into eighths or chunks.

Roast peppers on a rack in a broiler or over direct flame, turning often with tongs until they are charred on all sides. Place peppers in a plastic container or paper or plastic bag and cover. Allow peppers to steam inside the container for about 20 minutes. Then peel off the skin with your fingers, scraping off any stubborn pieces of peel with a knife blade. Do not wash the peppers if possible. A few flecks of peel are acceptable. Cut the peppers in half, remove the seeds and ribs and cut into strips about ½ inch wide.

Place walnuts on a baking sheet and toast in oven for about 7 to 10 minutes, then chop coarsely.

Toss the arugula with half the Garlic Vinaigrette and serve on a platter or on individual plates. Toss the peppers and onions with some of the remaining vinaigrette and place on top of the arugula. Top with toasted walnuts and optional crumbled feta cheese. Drizzle with remaining vinaigrette and serve immediately. You can make this salad without the arugula if you prefer.

GARLIC VINAIGRETTE

⅔ cup virgin olive oil
⅔ cup mild olive oil
⅓ cup red wine vinegar
1 tablespoon finely chopped garlic
2 teaspoons salt
2 teaspoons freshly ground black pepper

Combine all ingredients in a crock or bowl, and whisk.

Joyce Goldstein
Square One restaurant
Board Member of the American Institute of Wine and Food
San Francisco, California

CALIFORNIA WILD RICE SALAD
WITH PINE NUTS AND DRIED TOMATOES

This salad can be prepared a day ahead.

---

2 cups wild rice
3/4 cup pine nuts
1/4 cup sliced green olives with small amount of juice
2 ounces pimentos, chopped
1 cup chopped dried tomatoes
1/2 cup sliced red bell pepper
1/4 cup olive oil
3/4 cup red wine vinegar
fresh basil
rosemary
anise seed
Dijon mustard
black pepper

---

serves 2

Thoroughly wash the wild rice. Cook as directed, drain all water, set aside. Heat a 10 inch Calphalon omelette pan. Add a small amount of olive oil and sauté pine nuts until golden. Stir pine nuts into rice. Add the rest of the vegetables to the rice mixture. In a separate bowl, mix olive oil and red wine vinegar, season with spices and Dijon mustard to taste. In a large bowl, combine and toss dressing with rice/vegetable mixture. Chill at least 4 hours. Serve on oval platter with romaine lettuce, cut in long strips or "ribboned" as a decorative border around the rice.

Toni Douglas
The Broadway Southern California
Los Angeles, California

DUCK SALAD
WITH SEASONED VINAIGRETTE

Chicken or turkey can be substituted for duck in this light, refreshing salad.

---

2 cups duck meat, cooked
1 orange, peeled, sectioned
1 bunch romaine lettuce, washed, drained thoroughly
6 ounces spinach, washed, drained thoroughly
2 scallions, chopped
3/4 cup coarsely chopped pecans or walnuts
1 cup blueberries
1/4 cup Seasoned Vinaigrette
radish roses and extra blueberries for garnish

Slice duck meat into 2 inch long thin strips and reserve. Cut orange sections in half and set aside. In a large salad bowl, tear romaine and spinach into pieces. Toss in scallions, nuts, oranges, duck meat and blueberries. Make vinaigrette, and sprinkle over top of salad. Gently toss 10 times, until dressing coats ingredients. Serve on individual salad plates. Garnish with radish roses, and sprinkle a few blueberries around the plate.

SEASONED VINAIGRETTE

---

1 cup olive oil
1/2 cup corn oil
1/4 cup white wine vinegar, herbed
1 teaspoon sugar
dash of mustard
1 clove garlic, crushed
1 teaspoon oregano or tarragon
4 tablespoons mayonnaise

---

yields 1 3/4 cups

Place all ingredients in covered jar and shake briskly until blended.

Toula Patsalis
Kitchen Glamour
Detroit, Michigan

GAZPACHO SALAD

A wonderful salad for a summer day or to be enjoyed all year long. Use this dressing with its flavorful blend of seasonings for other salads.

DRESSING

½ cup olive oil
juice of 1 lime
1 large clove garlic, minced
1 tablespoon finely chopped onion
2 teaspoons finely chopped fresh cilantro (Chinese parsley)
¾ teaspoon salt
¼ teaspoon ground cayenne pepper
¼ teaspoon ground cumin
1 jalapeño pepper, minced
freshly ground black pepper

SALAD

1 large cucumber, peeled, sliced, quartered
1 small green bell pepper, cored, seeded, cut in strips
1 small yellow bell pepper, cored, seeded, cut in strips
3 medium ripe tomatoes, cut in chunks
1 large ripe avocado, peeled, cut in chunks, and tossed in lemon juice to prevent discoloring
1½ cups grated Monterey Jack cheese
½ cup sliced black olives, drained
broken tortilla chips

serves 8

Combine dressing ingredients and set aside. Put salad ingredients in a large bowl. Just before serving, toss with dressing. Sprinkle with broken tortilla chips for garnish and serve immediately.

Barbara Pool Fenzl
Les Gourmettes Cooking School
Food Editor, PHOENIX HOUSE AND GARDEN magazine
Board Member of the American Institute of Wine and Food
Phoenix, Arizona

GRILLED CHICKEN & GOAT CHEESE SALAD
WITH JALAPEÑO-CILANTRO-LIME SALSA

This beautifully arranged dish can easily be served as an entree. Substitute your favorite greens and sweet onions, if the ones suggested are not available.

---

6 chicken breast halves, boned, skin left on, wing bones attached
12 ounce log, fresh, California goat cheese, cut into 1/4 inch slices
salt and freshly ground black pepper
3 red bell peppers, stemmed, seeded, cut into 3/4 inch strips
3 yellow bell peppers, stemmed, seeded, cut into 3/4 inch strips
1 large Maui or sweet red onion peeled, cut into 3/8 inch slices
2 tablespoons extra virgin olive oil
3 heads limestone lettuce, leaves separated, washed, dried, torn in pieces
3 bunches mâche, leaves separated, washed, dried, torn in pieces
2 bunches arugula, leaves separated, washed, dried, torn in pieces
2 heads baby red leaf lettuce, leaves separated, washed, dried, torn in pieces
1 head baby radicchio, leaves separated
1 cup Tomato Concasse
1 cup Balsamic Vinaigrette
1 cup Jalapeño-Cilantro-Lime Salsa
1 bunch fresh chives, finely chopped

---

serves 6

Preheat grill or broiler. With finger, make a pocket between the skin and meat of each chicken breast, insert finger along the long side of each breast and leave the skin attached along the other edges. Insert goat cheese slices, overlapping slightly, inside the pockets to stuff the chicken breasts. Season the breasts with salt and pepper and set aside.

Brush pepper strips and onion slices with olive oil and season with salt and pepper, set aside.

Grill chicken breasts, skin side up first, until nicely browned, 3 to 5 minutes. Turn and grill for 5 to 7 minutes. About 1 minute before chicken is done, grill peppers and onion slices, about 30 seconds each side, until heated through and lightly charred. Arrange all the salad leaves on 6 large plates.

Cut each chicken breast crosswise into 4 or 5 slices and place in the center of a bed of greens. Garnish each plate with 3 spoonfuls of Tomato Concasse and the grilled peppers and onions. Dress the vegetables with the Balsamic Vinaigrette. Spoon the Salsa over the chicken. Sprinkle each serving with chopped chives.

TOMATO CONCASSE

4 medium tomatoes, peeled, cored, seeded, cut into 1/4 inch dice size pieces
1 cup extra virgin olive oil
1/4 cup sherry wine vinegar
1/2 medium shallot, finely chopped
2 tablespoons julienned fresh basil
salt and freshly ground white pepper

yields about 2 cups

Mix all ingredients in a bowl. Season with salt and pepper. Refrigerate covered for at least 30 minutes.

BALSAMIC VINAIGRETTE

1/3 cup balsamic vinegar
2/3 cup extra virgin olive oil
fresh lime juice
salt and freshly ground white pepper

yields 1 cup

Pour vinegar in a mixing bowl and whisk continuously, gradually adding olive oil. Season to taste with a little lime juice, salt and pepper.

JALAPEÑO-CILANTRO-LIME SALSA

2 jalapeño peppers, roasted, peeled, seeded and finely chopped
2 tablespoons chopped fresh cilantro leaves
1 cup extra virgin olive oil
salt and freshly ground white pepper
2 limes, cut in half

yields about 1 cup

Stir together jalapeños, cilantro and olive oil in a bowl. Season with salt and pepper. Just before serving, squeeze the limes into the mixture and stir well. (The lime juice will turn the cilantro brown if added any earlier.)

MICHAEL McCARTY
Michael's restaurant, Santa Monica, California and New York
Author of MICHAEL'S cookbook
Board Member of the American Institute of Wine and Food

GOAT CHEESE SALAD
WITH ARUGULA AND RADICCHIO WITH MUSTARD VINAIGRETTE DRESSING

It is important to use fresh goat cheese with this recipe because old goat cheese tastes rough and salty. Mâche is also known as lamb's lettuce.

---

4 ounces fresh chèvre (log shaped goat cheese), cut into 4 equal slices
1/4 cup extra virgin olive oil
1 1/2 teaspoons fresh thyme leaves
1 clove garlic, peeled, crushed
freshly ground pepper
2 small heads radicchio
1/2 pound arugula or mâche

---

serves 4

Put goat cheese in a bowl. Combine olive oil, 1 teaspoon thyme leaves, garlic and pepper to taste. Pour over cheese and marinate overnight.

Wash the radicchio and arugula and pat them dry with clean paper towels. Mix Mustard Vinaigrette Dressing. Toss salad greens in a bowl with dressing to coat lightly. Divide the greens on 4 large salad plates.

Heat a non-stick sauté pan until very hot and add 2 tablespoons of the goat cheese marinade. Sauté cheese over medium heat for 30 seconds on each side or place the cheese in a preheated 450 degree oven for 1 minute.

Top each salad with a slice of hot goat cheese. Garnish cheese with the remaining thyme leaves. Serve immediately.

MUSTARD VINAIGRETTE DRESSING

---

1 tablespoon Dijon Mustard
1 teaspoon finely chopped fresh tarragon
1 tablespoon sherry wine vinegar
salt and freshly ground white pepper
1 cup almond or extra virgin olive oil (or a mixture of both)

Combine mustard, tarragon, vinegar, salt and pepper in a small bowl. Slowly whisk in oil.

Correct the seasonings, including the mustard and vinegar, and reserve.

WOLFGANG PUCK
Spago California Cuisine, Chinois and Eureka restaurants
Author of THE WOLFGANG PUCK COOKBOOK
Los Angeles, California

OLD COUNTRY TABBOULEH

This recipe was Sally's grandmother's and comes from an area of Lebanon noted for its cooking. Tabbouleh can be served as a salad or as an appetizer. When serving it as an appetizer, place the tabbouleh in a bowl lined with the crisp inner lettuce leaves. Use the leaves to scoop and eat the tabbouleh.

½ cup fine bulghur (#1 cracked wheat)
2 large firm tomatoes, finely diced to minced
1 bunch green onions, minced
1 large cucumber, minced (optional)
4 small bunches parsley
½ cup olive oil
juice of 3 lemons
½ bunch mint (10 to 15 large leaves), minced or
2 tablespoons dried mint
1 tablespoon salt
½ teaspoon pepper

---

serves 4

Put bulghur in water, rinse and squeeze quickly so grain does not absorb too much water. Put bulghur in bowl and add tomatoes, onions and cucumber. Clean parsley by placing in a bowl and soaking in water 2 to 3 times. Use only the leafy area discarding as much of the stalk as possible, drain very well (doing this the night before cuts down preparation time), refrigerate dry. Chop parsley in a food processor, filling two-thirds full. Pulse 2 to 3 times, until parsley is chopped to ¼ to ⅜ inch pieces, do not mince, add to bulghur. To salad mixture, add oil first, then lemon, mint and salt and pepper to taste, it should be tangy. Mix well and let salad set until bulghur is no longer crunchy. Serve chilled.

Sally Hobbib Rumman
Sculptor and furniture designer
Sylvania, Ohio

ORIENTAL CHICKEN SALAD

2 whole chicken breasts, boned, skinned
1/4 cup chopped scallions
1/4 cup dry white wine
1/2 cup chicken broth
1/2 pound fresh snow peas
1 large red bell pepper
1 large yellow bell pepper
1 bunch scallions
1/2 cup cashew nuts

serves 4

Combine chopped scallions, white wine and chicken broth in a sauce pan and bring to a boil. Add chicken breasts, making sure they are covered with the liquid. Cover, bring to a boil and poach on lowest heat setting until breasts are no longer pink inside. Remove from heat, uncover, and allow to cool in juices.

Clean snow peas, pull off strings and blanch in boiling water for 30 seconds. Drain and cool peas in ice water, pat dry. Clean red and yellow peppers, cut in long strips. Slice scallions diagonally, including some greens. Cut cooled chicken breasts in slices. Mix chicken with all vegetables and cashew nuts in large bowl. Add salt and pepper lightly to taste, and chill.

To serve, pour Oriental Dressing over chicken mixture, toss lightly until well coated. Arrange salad on lettuce leaves.

ORIENTAL DRESSING

2 tablespoons dry sherry
1 1/2 tablespoons fresh lemon juice
1 tablespoon dry mustard
1 tablespoon soy sauce
1 teaspoon sugar
2 tablespoons sesame oil
1/4 cup vegetable oil
1/8 teaspoon cayenne pepper or hot red pepper flakes

Combine sherry, lemon juice, mustard, soy sauce and sugar in a bowl. Whisk until smooth. Continue whisking and add both oils. Season with pepper and mix well.

Ariana Kumpis
The Cookshop and Ariana's Cooking School
Member of the International Association of Culinary Professionals
Miami, Florida

RICE SHRIMP SALAD

Serve cold on a bed of lettuce garnished with parsley for lunch or light dinner on a warm day.

20 large shrimp
2 cups uncooked rice
3 cups chicken stock
2 cups chopped walnuts
½ cup chopped raisins
2 tablespoons chopped parsley
½ cup chopped scallions
½ cup chopped celery
½ cup chopped carrots
½ cup chopped green bell pepper
lettuce
parsley

serves 6-8

Shell, devein and cook shrimp, leave whole or chopped. Chill. Wash rice in sieve until water is clear. Place rice and chicken stock in heavy sauce pan. Boil hard for 2 to 3 minutes, then cover and reduce heat to lowest setting. Cook for 15 minutes or until all stock is absorbed, fluff with fork and cool.

Prepare the Lemon French Dressing. Combine rice with shrimp and remaining ingredients in a large salad bowl. Add the Lemon French Dressing and toss well. Serve salad cold on a bed of lettuce garnished with parsley.

LEMON FRENCH DRESSING

½ cup vegetable oil
½ cup olive oil
4 tablespoons lemon juice
½ teaspoon lemon peel
salt and freshly ground pepper

With a wire wisk, beat together the oils and lemon juice.

Whisk in lemon peel and salt and pepper to taste.

Madelyn Alvarez and Dinah Vince
Gourmet Grande, Inc.
Cleveland, Ohio

SPINACH SALAD

1/4 cup sugar
3 tablespoons vinegar
2 teaspoons horseradish
1/2 teaspoon dry mustard
8 ounces cottage cheese
8 ounces sour cream
1/2 cup chopped pecans
10 ounces fresh spinach, washed, dried thoroughly
pimentos (optional)

serves 8

Mix sugar and vinegar and set aside. Mix horseradish and mustard and set aside. Just before serving, mix all ingredients and toss with washed, dried spinach. Add chopped pimentos for a colorful accent, if desired. Serve at once.

Judith Thompson
Thompson's Office Supply & Gifts
El Reno, Oklahoma

WILD RICE SALAD
WITH CHICKEN AND CASHEWS

2½ cups cooked chicken or turkey
2½ cups cooked wild rice (about ¾ cup uncooked)
8 ounces pineapple chunks, drained
2 cups chopped celery
1 cup green grapes, halved
¾ cup coarsely chopped cashews or almonds
¾ cup mayonnaise
¾ cup chutney
½ teaspoon salt

---

serves 8-10

Cut chicken or turkey into bite size pieces. Toss rice, pineapple, celery, grapes, nuts and chicken together. Combine mayonnaise, chutney and salt. Blend all ingredients well. Cover and chill several hours before serving. Serve on lettuce leaves.

Donna Mathre
D. Mathre Gifts
Northfield, Minnesota

MAIN COURSES

BAY SCALLOPS
WITH PESTO SAUCE ON JAPANESE BUCKWHEAT NOODLES

BAY SCALLOPS

½ pound bay scallops
¼ cup olive oil
1 clove garlic, finely minced
1 tablespoon Pesto Sauce
1 tablespoon Parmesan cheese
juice of ½ lemon

serves 4

Lightly flour bay scallops and sprinkle with salt and pepper. Preheat a small pan to very hot and add olive oil. When oil is smoking slightly, sauté scallops and garlic quickly, about 3 seconds. Add Pesto Sauce, cheese and lemon juice, heat thoroughly.

On four warm plates, make a ring of Japanese Buckwheat Noodles and mound scallops in center. Garnish with basil and tarragon leaves.

PESTO SAUCE

2 cups basil leaves
1 teaspoon fresh tarragon leaves
1 tablespoon minced garlic
1 tablespoon pine nuts
½ cup olive oil
basil and tarragon leaves for garnish

Put ingredients in food processor. Process until smooth.

Store excess in tightly closed container.

JAPANESE BUCKWHEAT NOODLES

2¾ cups plus 2 tablespoons flour
½ cup minus 2 tablespoons buckwheat flour
1 whole egg
1 cup grated Japanese or Jersey red yam
pinch of salt
water

Combine flours in a medium mixing bowl. Work egg into combined flours. Add yam and salt. Add water if necessary. Knead for 20 minutes, then rest dough in refrigerator for 1 hour.

Put dough through pasta machine according to manufacturer's directions. Cut into spaghettini. Just before serving, cook in boiling water to al dente, about 2 minutes.

Yoshi Katsumura
Yoshi's Cafe
Chicago, Illinois

CHILLED POACHED SALMON
WITH DILL YOGURT SAUCE

Poaching is a healthy way to enjoy fish. Use a whole salmon, filet or steaks as suggested, adjusting the cooking time according to the size. The fresh dill flavor of the creamy yogurt sauce complements the chilled fish.

---

6 salmon steaks
4 cups white wine
4 cups water
2 bay leaves
1 teaspoon thyme
1/4 cup chopped fresh parsley with stems
1 cup finely chopped celery
1 cup finely chopped carrots
1/2 cup finely chopped onions
1/4 teaspoon black pepper

---

serves 6

In a Calphalon 20 inch fish poacher, combine white wine, water, bay leaves, thyme, parsley, celery, carrots, onions and pepper. Bring to a full boil for 15 minutes and then reduce to a low simmer. Place salmon steaks on poaching rack. Insert rack with salmon into poacher and cover. Poach for 10 to 12 minutes depending on salmon thickness. Remove salmon steaks from poacher and chill. Serve with Dill Yogurt Sauce and garnish with a sprig of fresh dill and a lemon slice.

DILL YOGURT SAUCE

---

1 cup lowfat yogurt
1 tablespoon finely chopped fresh dill weed
1/4 teaspoon finely chopped fresh thyme
1/8 teaspoon white pepper

Drain off excess water from yogurt. Fold in spices and chill.

Paul Angelo LoGiudice
Culinary Events Specialist
Commercial Aluminum Cookware Company

CRABMEAT QUESADILLAS

Use this dish as an entree, first course, or hors d'oeuvre. Serve with your favorite fresh salsa or with the Jalapeño-Cilantro-Lime Salsa.

½ cup Muenster cheese, grated
½ cup Monterey Jack cheese, grated
2 tablespoons Parmesan cheese, grated
¼ cup goat cheese
1 cup crabmeat, steamed, shredded
4 8-inch flour tortillas
peanut oil
salsa

serves 2-4

Combine cheeses in food processor by mixing in short pulses, turning processor on and off until cheese mixture is crumbly in texture.

Assemble quesadillas by placing ¼ cup of cheese mixture in the middle of the tortilla. Top with ¼ cup of crabmeat. Fold the tortilla gently in half, making sure the cheese filling stays in the middle.

Preheat a Calphalon crêpe pan, or griddle on medium heat. Wipe the interior with a paper towel moistened with peanut oil. Place folded tortilla in pan and cook for approximately 1 minute on each side, allowing the cheese to melt and the outside to become slightly crisp. Repeat for remaining tortillas. Cut into four wedges and serve with fresh salsa.

pictured
paella, 133
grilled chicken & goat cheese salad, 44
grilled tuna in ginger-cilantro butter sauce, 68

PAUL ANGELO LOGIUDICE
Culinary Events Specialist
Commercial Aluminum Cookware Company

FETTUCCINE
WITH SMOKED SALMON

Vary this recipe by substituting the smoked salmon with smoked fish, turkey, ham or steamed chicken.

---

2 cups dried fettuccine, broken into pieces
4 cups chicken broth or water
1 teaspoon salt
6 tablespoons butter
1 clove garlic, crushed
1/3 cup chopped fresh chives or scallions, or 2 tablespoons dried
2 tablespoons fresh thyme, or 1 teaspoon dried
1/2 teaspoon pepper
1/2 pound smoked salmon or chubb, cut in bite size pieces
1/2 cup light sour cream
1/2 cup grated fontinella

---

serves 6

In a 5 quart pot, bring chicken broth and salt to a rolling boil. Add noodles and stir well. Reduce heat to medium and cook until tender, about 15 minutes. Drain in a colander.

Melt butter in a large skillet. Sauté garlic, chives and thyme, stir well. Toss the noodles with the herbed butter and cook over medium heat for 2 minutes. Add pepper, smoked salmon pieces, then dot with sour cream. Stir and toss gently over medium heat. Transfer to a platter and sprinkle with grated fontinella.

Toula Patsalis
Kitchen Glamour
Member of the International Association of Culinary Professionals
Detroit, Michigan

SCALLOPS PAPRIKASH

This recipe works equally well by stubstituting veal scallops, pounded thin and cut into 1 inch slices. Sauté some mushrooms and red and green peppers with the veal, and omit the final addition of butter. Sprinkle the parsley on top before serving.

---

1 pound scallops
4 tablespoons butter
2 tablespoons olive oil
3 cloves garlic, minced
½ teaspoon salt
⅛ teaspoon freshly ground black pepper
1 teaspoon medium Hungarian paprika
3 tablespoons chopped parsley
3 tablespoons lemon juice

---

serves 4

Wash and dry scallops removing all traces of sand. In a large 3 quart sauté pan, heat 2 tablespoons of butter and olive oil. Sauté the garlic gently for 2 minutes, then add salt, pepper and paprika. Turn up the heat and sauté the scallops, stirring occasionally until done, 5 to 10 minutes. Remove from pan and place on serving plate.

Add the parsley, lemon juice and remaining butter to the same pan. Cook until the butter is melted, and pour over scallops. Sprinkle with additional parsley before serving.

David Kobos
The Kobos Company
Portland, Oregon

PIZZA
WITH SMOKED SALMON AND GOLDEN CAVIAR

1 recipe Basic Pizza Dough
3 to 4 ounces smoked salmon
1 tablespoon minced chives
4 tablespoons extra virgin olive oil
6 tablespoons sour cream or crème fraîche
4 heaping tablespoons domestic golden caviar
1 heaping teaspoon black caviar

makes 4 pizzas

Preheat oven to 500 degrees and place a pizza stone inside for 30 minutes prior to baking pizzas.

Cut salmon into paper thin slices. Reserve.

On a lightly floured surface, knead 2 teaspoons minced chives into the Basic Pizza Dough. Roll or stretch dough into four 8 inch circles leaving edges thicker than the center. Place the pizzas on a lightly floured wooden baker's peel. Brush the centers of the circles to within 1 inch of the edge with olive oil. Slide pizza crusts onto the stone and bake 8 to 10 minutes. When they are golden brown, transfer them from the oven to a serving plate.

Spread each pizza with sour cream. Arrange the slices of salmon decoratively over the sour cream. Place a spoonful of golden caviar in the center of each pizza, then spoon a little of the black caviar into the center of the golden caviar. Sprinkle the salmon with the remaining chives. Place the pizzas on heated dinner plates and serve immediately.

BASIC PIZZA DOUGH

You can also roll out the pizzas with a rolling pin, then inch up the edges with your fingers to form a slight ridge.

---

1 package fresh or dry yeast
1/4 cup warm water
1 teaspoon salt
1 tablespoon honey
2 tablespoons olive oil
3/4 cup cool water
3 cups flour

Dissolve yeast in 1/4 cup warm water and let proof for 10 minutes. Combine the salt, honey, olive oil and the 3/4 cup cool water in a bowl. Mix well. Place the flour in a food processor.

With the motor running, slowly pour the salt and the honey liquid through the feed tube. Then pour in the dissolved yeast. Process until the dough forms a ball on the blade. If it is sticky, add small amounts of flour.

Transfer the dough to a lightly floured surface and knead until smooth. Place in a buttered bowl and allow the dough to rest, covered, for 30 minutes.

Divide the dough into four equal parts. Roll each piece into a smooth, tight ball. Place on a flat sheet or dish, cover with a damp towel and refrigerate up to 6 hours.

One hour before baking, remove the dough from the refrigerator and let it come to room temperature.

WOLFGANG PUCK
Spago California Cuisine, Chinois and Eureka restaurants
Author of THE WOLFGANG PUCK COOKBOOK
Los Angeles, California

SPICY SHRIMP

½ cup corn or safflower oil
⅓ cup minced onion
1 tablespoon minced garlic
1 tablespoon plus 1 teaspoon minced fresh ginger
¼ cup plus 2 tablespoons chicken stock or broth
½ teaspoon Tabasco sauce
1½ pounds large unshelled shrimp (about 45)
salt

---

serves 4

Heat ¼ cup of oil until hot in a medium Dutch oven or heavy wide sauce pan. Sauté onion stirring constantly, until it starts to brown, about 6 minutes, do not burn. Add the garlic and ginger and sauté, stirring frequently, for 5 minutes. Pour in stock and Tabasco and boil 30 seconds.

Turn off heat and stir in remaining ¼ cup of oil. Add shrimp, tossing to coat thoroughly with seasoning mixture. Let stand at room temperature 20 minutes or up to 3 hours in refrigerator, covered.

Stir shrimp occasionally. Remove shrimp from refrigerator 30 minutes before serving.

Before serving, place covered Dutch oven over medium high heat. Cook shrimp, stirring frequently and recovering pan until shrimp are just cooked through, 5 to 7 minutes. Do not overcook. Season with salt and Tabasco.

Divide shrimp and sauce into 4 bowls and serve immediately with crusty bread for dipping.

Betty Boote
Managing Editor, HOUSE BEAUTIFUL magazine
New York, New York

TOM'S CRAB CAKES

Phil Margolis, a longtime friend of Ron's, sent this anecdote –"I remember once when Ron was in New York, and he got in the mood for good Maryland crab cakes. You can get about anything in New York (at any hour, delivered) but you can't get good crab cakes. Ron called, and I met him on 'Air Calphalon' at a private hanger at Philadelphia's airport with 12 piping hot crab cakes from Philadelphia's famous Maryland style crab house, DiNardos."

---

1 pound lump crabmeat
dash of sea salt
freshly ground black pepper
1 tablespoon Worcestershire sauce
1 teaspoon "Old Bay Seasoning"
2 large eggs, beaten
1/3 cup plain bread crumbs
2 tablespoons butter

---

serves 6

With a fork, blend all ingredients except butter. Form mixture into 6 three inch cakes. In a preheated 5 quart Calphalon sauté pan, add the butter. When butter starts to bubble, add crab cakes. Cook over medium heat until golden brown on both sides.

Tom Shenk
Kellen Company
Annandale, Virginia

GRILLED TUNA
IN GINGER-CILANTRO BUTTER SAUCE

---

4 tuna filets, 6 ounces each
Asian Barbecue Marinade
2/3 cup dry white wine
1/4 cup white wine vinegar
1 tablespoon finely minced fresh ginger
1 small shallot, minced
1 cup unsalted butter, at room temperature
1 teaspoon grated or minced lemon peel
1/4 cup finely minced cilantro (fresh coriander)
1/4 teaspoon or more freshly ground white pepper
1/4 teaspoon salt

---

serves 4

Marinate tuna in Asian Barbecue Marinade for 1 hour. Remove tuna and reserve marinade.

While the tuna is marinating begin preparing the Ginger-Cilantro Butter sauce. Place the wine, vinegar, ginger and shallot in a small saucepan and bring to a rapid boil over high heat and cook until four tablespoons remain. Set aside. Cut the butter into 16 pieces and set aside.

If using a gas barbecue, preheat to medium (350 degrees). If using charcoal or wood, prepare the fire. When the coal or wood is ash covered, place the fish in a grilling basket. Grill over medium high heat until they begin to flake, about 8 minutes. Turn once during barbecuing and brush with the reserved marinade. Transfer fish to heated dinner plates or a serving platter.

Bring the wine and vinegar sauce to a rapid boil over medium high heat, then add butter all at once and beat vigorously with a whisk, about 20 seconds, or until just a few lumps of butter remain. Pour sauce into a bowl. Stir in the lemon peel, cilantro, pepper and salt. Taste and adjust the seasonings, adding more pepper if necessary. Spoon the sauce around the fish and serve at once.

ASIAN BARBECUE MARINADE

This marinade is equally delicious used with other grilled fish or chicken.

¼ cup sherry
¼ cup light soy sauce
2 tablespoons oyster sauce
2 tablespoons lemon juice
2 tablespoons Oriental sesame oil
½ teaspoon freshly ground black pepper
1 bunch chives, minced
¼ cup finely minced fresh ginger

Combine all ingredients, blend well.

Hugh Carpenter
Chopstix restaurants
Author of CHOPSTIX and PACIFIC FLAVORS cookbooks
Member of the International Association of Culinary Professionals
Los Angeles, California

TRUITE BOURGUIGNONNE

While traveling in the Burgundy wine area of France in 1979, Ron met Monsieur Marc Chevillot, a fellow member of the Confre Rie des Chevaliers du Tastevin. While there, Monsieur Chevillot served him this delicious trout dish. Ron enjoyed it so much that he took the recipe back to the Toledo Chapter, where it was served at the "Paulée de Meursault" (a celebration of the season's first crop).

---

7 pound trout
3 liters of good, strong red wine
6 carrots, sliced
4 onions, sliced
2 whole garlic, peeled, sliced
6 parsley sprigs
½ bay leaf
3 teaspoons salt
10 to 12 white peppercorns, ground

---

serves 8

Prepare a Red Court Bouillon by combining wine, carrots, onions, garlic, parsley, bay leaf, salt and peppercorns. Bring to a boil and cook for 15 minutes.

Reduce heat to a simmer and poach the trout for 8 minutes. Poach the trout only half submerged in the Red Court Bouillon so it will become a deep wine color on the bottom and lighter on top. Serve with the Beurre Blanc.

BEURRE BLANC

---

3 to 4 shallots, sliced
1 cup white Chablis wine
1½ cups melted sweet butter
1 cup heavy cream
salt and pepper

Bring wine and shallots to a boil over medium high heat. Reduce by one third.

Whisk butter into wine mixture. Stir in cream. Season with salt and pepper.

MONSIEUR MARC CHEVILLOT
Hôtel de la Poste
Beaune, France

WHITEFISH
WITH SOUR ORANGE SAUCE

---

2 pounds whitefish filets
½ cup plus 2 teaspoons flour
6 tablespoons butter
2 tablespoons olive oil
6 tablespoons shallots, minced
2 cups fresh squeezed orange juice with pulp
½ cup fresh squeezed lemon juice with pulp
salt and pepper

---

serves 4

Dredge fish in ½ cup flour. Preheat a Calphalon oval flambé pan on medium heat. When pan is hot, add 2 tablespoons butter. When butter is bubbling briskly, add oil and heat another minute. Cook fish for 2 to 5 minutes on each side. Cooking time will vary depending on the thickness of the filet. Fish should flake easily and be opaque; if fish is cooked too long it will fall apart. When fish is done use a flexible metal spatula to remove fish from the pan, taking care to release the delicate coating from the pan. Set fish aside and keep warm.

Drain excess oil from the pan. Add 4 tablespoons butter and heat until bubbling briskly. Cook shallots for 1 minute. Add 2 teaspoons of flour to butter and shallots, and stir for 1 minute. Stir in orange and lemon juices. Bring to a boil and reduce mixture to one half the amount, stirring occasionally. Season with salt and pepper. Serve over fish.

Paul Angelo LoGiudice
Culinary Events Specialist
Commercial Aluminum Cookware Company

BEEF TENDERLOIN RAGOÛT

2 pounds tenderloin tips, cut into 3/4 inch pieces
1/4 cup butter
1 tablespoon flour
1 clove garlic, minced
4 cups beef stock
1 cup burgundy wine
1 cup water
pinch of pepper
1 1/2 teaspoons salt
1 bay leaf
1/4 teaspoon ground marjoram
1 cup fresh mushrooms, cut in half
6 small whole onions,
1/4 cup sliced water chestnuts
6 artichoke hearts, halved

serves 6

Preheat oven to 325 degrees. Sauté beef in butter until browned. Stir in flour and garlic, then transfer to roast pan.

Combine beef stock, wine, water, pepper, salt, bay leaf and marjoram. Pour over beef. Cover roast pan and bake for 1 1/2 hours or until beef is done. Add mushrooms and onions to roast pan and return to oven until mushrooms are just tender. Just before serving, add water chestnuts and artichoke hearts. Serve with noodles seasoned with parsley.

Courtesy of Jim Stirratt, George Collins, Karen Dodge
Dayton's Marshall Field's Hudson's
Minneapolis, Minnesota

CHILES RELLENOS CASSEROLE

This is a good dish to serve for brunch since it can be made ahead. Use your own favorite tomato sauce or try Jeff's Favorite Tomato and Garlic Sauce.

---

8 ounces canned, whole green chilies
1 pound ground beef
1 large onion, chopped
2 cloves garlic, crushed
3 tablespoons chili mix
1 teaspoon cumin powder
8 ounces Monterey Jack cheese, grated
8 ounces cheddar cheese, grated
13 ounces evaporated milk
4 eggs, beaten
1 tablespoon flour
favorite tomato sauce

---

serves 8

Grease an 8x13 inch casserole dish. Rinse chilies, cut and open out, remove seeds and drain on paper towel. Brown ground beef, onions and garlic in large omelette pan. Stir in seasonings. Combine cheeses in a separate bowl and set aside. In the prepared dish, make a single layer of half the chilies, layer beef mixture and then top with remaining chilies. Sprinkle with the cheese mixture. In another bowl, whisk evaporated milk and eggs, add flour, beating until mixed. Pour egg mixture over cheese. Dish can be prepared ahead to this point and refrigerated until ready to cook.

When ready to bake, preheat oven to 350 degrees. Lightly cover the casserole with tomato sauce. Bake in oven until edges begin to brown and casserole looks set and firm. Cut into squares and garnish with raisins and pecans. Serve with sour cream.

MARY JEAN MCDANIEL
Walter Davis, Inc.
Dallas, Texas

BRACIOLE RIPIENCE
CON SALSA DI POMODORO
STUFFED MEAT ROLL WITH TOMATO SAUCE

This recipe is one that Paul borrowed from his family's traditional Italian Easter dinner. Paul had to interpret the recipe since his grandmother, like most grandmothers, did not record her recipes.

---

3 top round steaks, 1/4 inch thick
3 small hard boiled eggs, quartered
9 slices hard salami
3 tablespoons fresh chopped parsley
1/4 pound provolone cheese, sliced
1/2 cup chopped scallions
3/4 cup Parmesan cheese, grated
black pepper
2 tablespoons olive oil
1/2 cup red wine
Salsa di Pomodoro

---

serves 6

Prepare Salsa di Pomodoro at least one hour ahead.

Place steaks on parchment paper. Cover with another piece of parchment paper and pound to 1/8 inch thick. Remove top sheet of parchment paper. Season with pepper. Place quarters of egg in a row on short end of each steak. Distribute salami slices, parsley, scallions and provolone cheese over remaining portion of each steak. Sprinkle with Parmesan cheese and black pepper. Starting at the end with the egg, roll up each steak very tightly and tie with cooking twine.

Preheat a Calphalon 3 quart sauté pan on medium heat. Add olive oil to preheated pan. Sauté meat rolls until thoroughly browned. Remove and place in the simmering Salsa di Pomodoro. Deglaze pan by pouring in 1/2 cup red wine. Using a metal spatula, release any meat drippings still remaining, reduce by one half, then pour mixture into sauce. Cover and simmer braciole in sauce 3 to 4 hours.

SALSA DI POMODORO

---

4 tablespoons olive oil
3 cloves garlic, minced
2 medium onions, chopped
2 28-ounce cans peeled, crushed tomatoes
6 ounces tomato paste
3 cups water
1 teaspoon salt
2 teaspoons ground pepper
1 tablespoon basil
2 tablespoons oregano
1 teaspoon sugar

Preheat a Calphalon 5 quart saucier pan. Add 1 tablespoon olive oil. Heat for 1 minute. Sauté onions and garlic for 3 minutes, then add remaining ingredients. Bring to a boil, reduce to low heat and simmer for 1 hour. Additional water may be added as sauce cooks down.

Paul Angelo LoGiudice
Culinary Events Specialist
Commercial Aluminum Cookware Company

GAISBURGER MARSCH

This traditional eintopf (stew) from Württemberg is named after a local historical conflict in which, according to folklore, all the men from Gaisburg were taken prisoner. Their wives were allowed to bring the men their meals. However, the women were permitted only one bowl or pot for each man. Each Frau packed her one pot with nourishing ingredients - meat, broth, bones with marrow, vegetables, spätzle - and delivered the eintopf piping hot. The men stayed well fed until the conflict was settled. Today, many of Germany's decorated chefs include the Gaisburger Marsch on their menus. Ask your butcher to bone the meat and cut in 2½ inch lengths.

---

6 pound beef shank, boned (about 4 pounds of meat)
1 beef shank bone, about 2 pounds
4 tablespoons butter
2 onions, sliced
2 teaspoons dried marjoram
salt and freshly ground black pepper
6 quarts water
2 carrots, halved, quartered
1 parsnip, halved, quartered
2 cloves garlic, peeled, bruised
1 whole onion, peeled
4 bay leaves
4 stalks celery, quartered

---

serves 16

Melt the butter in a large soup pot. Add the meat and brown on all sides. Remove meat with a slotted spoon and set aside. Add the sliced onions and cook until golden brown, about 8 minutes. Add the marjoram and season with salt and pepper.

Return meat to the soup pot. Add the water, carrots, parsnip, garlic, whole onion, bay leaves and celery. Heat on high to boiling, reduce heat, and simmer, covered, for 1 hour. Add the bones and simmer for 1 hour more.

Using a slotted spoon, transfer meat, bones and vegetables to a plate. Allow broth to cool, then skim fat.

Cut the meat into 2 inch pieces. Heat the broth to boiling and add the meat and vegetables. Reduce heat and simmer until meat is warmed through, about 5 minutes. Just before serving, add a generous portion of spätzle.

RUTH AND SKITCH HENDERSON
Silo, Inc.
Authors of SEASONS IN THE COUNTRY cookbook
Ruth is a member of the International Association of Culinary Professionals
New Milford, Connecticut

PICADILLO, CUBAN STYLE

There are as many variations of "picadillo" as there are Cuban cooks. Some recipes call for ground beef, pork or ham, or a mixture of all three.

1/4 cup vegetable oil
1 large onion, minced
1 large green pepper, minced
2 large cloves garlic, minced
1 1/2 pounds lean ground beef
1/2 cup raisins
1/2 cup salad size olives with red pimento centers, chopped
1 tablespoon capers (optional)
8 ounces tomato sauce
1/2 cup dry sherry or dry vermouth
salt and pepper

---

serves 6

In a large omelette or sauté pan heat oil. Sauté onions, pepper and garlic until onion is translucent. Do not brown.

Stir in ground beef and cook until brown and crumbly. Drain excess oil. Add remaining ingredients. Season with salt and pepper. Cover, cook over low heat, about 15 to 20 minutes. Serve over white fluffy rice.

SONIA R. PEREZ
The Kitchen Shop, Inc.
Miami Lakes, Florida

RANCH CHILI
WITH JALAPEÑO CORN BREAD

The exact origin of chili is not known although there are many folklore stories. When Paul developed this recipe he discovered that traditional chili contained suet for flavor, no beans, and unground pieces of beef and pork.

---

4 dried Anaheim chili peppers
4 jalapeño chili peppers, roasted, peeled, seeds and veins removed
½ cup chopped suet
2 pounds beef chuck roast, cut into ½ inch cubes
1 pound coarse ground pork
2 large onions, chopped
3 cloves garlic, finely chopped
1 green bell pepper, chopped
2 cups beef broth
28 ounce can whole tomatoes, chopped
6 ounces tomato paste
½ teaspoon Tabasco sauce
1 tablespoon cumin, freshly ground
1 tablespoon Mexican oregano
1 teaspoon paprika
salt and pepper
2 tablespoons masa harina (corn flour)

---

serves 8

Bring 3 cups water to a boil in a Calphalon 2½ quart sauce pan. Add dried Anaheim chili peppers. Reduce heat, cover and simmer for 30 minutes. Remove peppers from water and set water aside for later use. Cut peppers open and discard seeds, vein and stem. Lay peppers on cutting board, skin side down, scrape flesh of pepper off skin. Discard skin. Finely chop Anaheim peppers and jalapeño peppers.

Preheat a Calphalon 3 quart sauté pan on medium heat. When pan is hot, add ¼ cup suet. Melt fat, remove any unmelted suet bits. Add chopped beef chuck roast and brown on all sides. While searing meat, strain and reserve excess liquid for later use. When beef is nicely browned, remove from pan. Add pork and follow the above directions for browning. Remove pork and set aside with beef. Deglaze pan by pouring 1 cup of beef stock into pan. Using a flat-edged metal spatula, loosen meat drippings from the pan's surface. Reduce liquid to one half the amount.

Meanwhile, preheat a Calphalon 8 quart stock pot on medium heat. Add ¼ cup suet, melt fat and remove suet bits. Sauté onion, garlic and bell peppers until onions are translucent. Add tomatoes, tomato paste, chili peppers, Tabasco, cumin, oregano and paprika. Season with salt and pepper. Stir in browned beef and pork. Pour in beef stock, liquid from browning meat, and reserved pepper water. Bring chili to a boil. Reduce heat to maintain a simmer for 2 to 3 hours. Do not cover. If liquid reduces too much, add water. Skim off excess fat. Mix masa harina with 1/4 cup of water, then stir into chili. Cook for another 30 minutes. Serve hot with Jalapeño Corn Bread.

JALAPEÑO CORN BREAD

1 1/2 teaspoons baking powder
3 cups yellow cornmeal
1 cup unbleached flour
1 teaspoon baking soda
3 tablespoons sugar
3/4 teaspoon salt
3 large eggs
2 1/4 cups buttermilk
1 1/2 cups cooked corn
3 jalapeño peppers, finely chopped, seeds and veins removed
1 tablespoon butter

serves 8

Preheat oven to 400 degrees. In oven, heat a Calphalon 9x13 inch oval au gratin pan.

Combine dry ingredients in a large bowl. In a separate bowl whisk eggs, then blend in buttermilk. Using a spatula, fold the liquid mixture into the dry ingredients. Stir only until blended, do not over mix. Fold corn and jalapeño peppers into mixture.

Remove pan from oven. Place butter in pan, allow it to melt, then coat the surface and sides of pan. Pour batter into pan and bake for 30 to 35 minutes. Cool and serve directly from pan.

Paul Angelo LoGiudice
Culinary Events Specialist
Commercial Aluminum Cookware Company

MEXICAN SALPICON

This southwestern dish gets its flavor from the fresh cilantro, also known as coriander, which is related to the parsley family. Lime juice can be used as a substitute, or in combination with the vinegar.

---

3 pound beef brisket
2 onions, 1 halved, 1 chopped
1 large carrot, quartered
1 stalk celery, quartered
2 cloves garlic
1 cup chopped fresh cilantro
12 ounce can whole tomatoes
salt and pepper
1 large tomato, chopped
4 ounces chili chipotle peppers, drained, chopped (reserve liquid)
¼ cup light olive oil
¼ cup vinegar
½ pound Monterey Jack cheese, cut in ¼ inch cubes
2 large avocados, sliced lengthwise

---

serves 15

Put beef brisket in an 8 quart saucier and cover with water. Add halved onion, carrot, celery, garlic, ½ cup chopped cilantro and canned tomatoes. Season with salt and pepper. Cover and simmer for 4 hours until very tender.

Remove beef brisket from pan, cool and then shred thoroughly with a fork. In a large bowl combine the shredded beef, chopped onion, chopped tomato, remaining cilantro, chopped chili chipotle, oil and vinegar. Season to taste with the chili chipotle liquid and salt and pepper. Refrigerate for at least 4 hours. Toss with cheese before serving and garnish with avocado slices. Serve with warm corn or flour tortillas and pinto beans.

Mary Jean McDaniel
Walter Davis, Inc.
Dallas, Texas

VEAL CHOPS
WITH CANDIED LEMON ZEST AND GINGER

Ron enjoyed going to Yoshi's to experience his wonderful blending of Far Eastern and Western cooking.

---

4 veal chops
6 ounces fresh ginger root, peeled, finely julienned
zest of 3 lemons, finely julienned
water
1 cup sugar
1 quart Madeira
7 to 10 shallots, finely chopped
2 cups veal stock
salt and pepper
butter

---

serves 4

Blanch ginger and lemon zest in boiling water for 10 seconds. Set aside.

Bring 1 cup of water and sugar to boil in a sauce pan, reduce to a syrup. Add blanched ginger and lemon zest, cook for 5 minutes. Set aside.

Bring Madeira and shallots to a boil in a sauce pan and reduce to a glaze. Stir in veal stock, bring to a simmer, and strain. Season with salt and pepper, add butter to taste.

Sauté veal chops in butter over medium high heat, 3 to 4 minutes per side. Do not overcook, veal chops should be medium rare to medium. Remove veal chops to warm plates. Pour sauce around the chops and garnish with lemon zest and ginger. Fresh pasta is an excellent accompaniment.

Chef Yoshi Katsumura
Yoshi's Cafe
Chicago, Illinois

BUTTERFLIED LEG OF LAMB
WITH THYME-MUSTARD MARINADE

This is a favorite of the Segal family, when they are at their Wisconsin country home. For a perfect summer meal, we recommend serving this delicious lamb with California Wild Rice Salad and Strawberry Rhubarb Betty.

---

7 to 8 pound butterflied leg of lamb
2/3 cup extra virgin olive oil
1 tablespoon fresh thyme
1/4 cup stone ground mustard
1/4 cup lemon juice
1/2 teaspoon dried ginger
5 large cloves garlic, peeled
3 shallots, peeled
1 teaspoon salt
freshly ground pepper

---

serves 10

Put lamb in a very large china or glass container. Place remainder of ingredients in food processor and process for 15 seconds, until garlic and shallots are minced. Pour marinade over lamb. Cover with plastic wrap and refrigerate overnight. Turn occasionally. The next day, bring lamb to room temperature. Prepare grill and grill about 10 minutes on each side for rare. Slice thinly.

Gordon and Carole Segal
Crate and Barrel
Northbrook, Illinois

UPHOLSTERED LEG OF LAMB

The dried ancho chili pepper seeds provide the "fire" in this dish.

4 pound leg of lamb
6 dried ancho chili peppers
2 cloves garlic, slivered
salt and pepper
2 medium tomatoes, peeled, seeded, quartered
1 large onion, chopped
1 teaspoon sugar
2 tablespoons lard or corn oil
2 cups chicken stock
rice

serves 8

To prepare the chili peppers, pull off the stems and the core. Remove the veins and the seeds reserving as many seeds as your palate enjoys. Wash the chili peppers in cold water, tear them into pieces, and soak these in 1 cup hot water for about 20 minutes.

Make 6 incisions in the leg of lamb and insert garlic slivers. Season the lamb with salt and pepper. Place the lamb in a heavy casserole with a lid. Preheat oven to 300 degrees.

Put the quartered tomatoes, onions, chili peppers with seeds and their water and sugar in a blender. Blend to a coarse puree. Sauté puree in lard or corn oil for 5 minutes, stirring constantly. Add the chicken stock and mix with the puree. Pour the sauce over the leg of lamb. Seal the casserole with aluminum foil, then cover with the lid. Cook for 3½ hours. Serve with rice which has been cooked in equal parts of water and sauce from the lamb casserole.

Wendy Condon
Walter Davis Inc.
Dallas, Texas

RACK OF LAMB
WITH ROSEMARY AND ARTICHOKES

Have your butcher trim the lamb and give you the bones and trimmings for the lamb stock. Allow the lamb to rest after roasting so the juices are distributed evenly throughout the meat. Create a mirepoix with equal parts of coarsely chopped carrots, onions and celery.

---

1 pound rack of baby lamb
freshly ground pepper
1 small sprig rosemary, plus ½ teaspoon chopped rosemary
1 to 2 tablespoons extra virgin olive oil
1 cup mirepoix
½ teaspoon whole black peppercorns
½ bay leaf
salt
4 fresh artichoke bottoms, cooked
juice of 1 lemon
4 tablespoons unsalted butter
1 sprig fresh thyme, leaves only
12 cloves garlic, peeled, blanched

---

serves 2

Trim all but a thin layer of fat from the lamb. Cut off the last 2 inches of the rib bones. Reserve all the trimmings. Rub the rack with pepper and the rosemary sprig, then rub it with olive oil. Cover the rack with plastic wrap and refrigerate overnight.

To make lamb stock, brown the cut lamb bones and trimmings in a little olive oil. Add the mirepoix and brown for 2 to 3 minutes. Add the peppercorns and bay leaf. Add water to cover, bring to a boil and simmer slowly until the stock is reduced to ½ cup. Strain and reserve.

Preheat the oven to 450 degrees. Place the lamb in a shallow roasting pan and season with salt. Roast the rack for 10 to 12 minutes, or until the lamb is medium rare. Transfer the lamb to a carving board and let it rest in a warm spot for 10 minutes.

Slice the artichoke bottoms into thin slices and toss them with lemon juice. In a sauté pan, in 2 tablespoons of butter, slowly sauté the artichoke slices with the thyme leaves, and 2 of the garlic cloves cut into thin slices. Season with salt and pepper. Cook until artichokes are tender, adding more butter if necessary. Reserve.

While the lamb is resting, discard any grease from the roasting pan. Deglaze the pan with the lamb stock. Add the chopped rosemary. When the sauce has reduced slightly, whisk in 1 tablespoon of the butter. Season the sauce with salt and pepper and strain. Keep the sauce warm.

Heat a sauté pan, add the remaining butter and sauté the remaining garlic cloves until light golden brown. Slice the lamb into chops. Arrange them attractively on warm dinner plates. Surround with the artichokes. Spoon the sauce over the lamb and scatter the cloves of garlic randomly over the artichoke slices.

Wolfgang Puck
Spago California Cuisine, Chinois and Eureka restaurants
Author of THE WOLFGANG PUCK COOKBOOK
Los Angeles, California

JOEY'S SAVORY PORK CHOPS

This is a simple and enjoyable recipe that has good basic flavors. A beginning cook would find this an excellent choice to serve to family and friends.

---

5 to 6 pork chops
2 tablespoons oil
¼ cup white wine
1 cup chicken broth
1 tablespoon butter
6 radishes, thinly sliced
1 medium onion, thinly sliced
½ green pepper, cut in strips
1 clove garlic, minced

---

serves 4-6

Brown pork chops in hot oil in a 5 quart sauté pan. Reduce heat and pour in wine and chicken broth. Cover and simmer for 15 to 20 minutes or until tender.

Ten minutes before pork chops are done, melt butter over medium heat in a 10 inch sauté pan. Sauté radishes, onion, pepper and garlic until vegetables are crisp or tender to taste. When pork chops are nearly finished, pour vegetable mixture over pork chops and broth. Serve with pasta or rice.

Terry G. Fewell
That Cook 'N' Coffee Place
West Dundee, Illinois

PORK TENDERLOIN
WITH BROCCOLI IN PLUM SAUCE

This dish can be varied by substituting pea pods or other green vegetables for broccoli. Shoyu is what the Japanese call soy sauce. Chinese plum sauce and oyster sauce can be purchased at any Chinese market or in most supermarkets in the Oriental food section.

---

1 pork tenderloin, approximately 1 pound
Plum Sauce Marinade
1 bunch broccoli, stems peeled and cut off, broken into small pieces
1 red pepper, sliced
1 onion, cut into wedges (preferably a mild type)
sesame oil
peanut oil

---

serves 2-4

Cut pork tenderloin into ½ inch slices. Pour Plum Sauce Marinade over pork slices and marinate for 2 hours or overnight.

Preheat 12 inch flat bottom wok. Add 1 to 2 teaspoons peanut oil. Stir fry vegetables in peanut oil, begin with onion, then add broccoli and red pepper. Remove vegetables from pan when just cooked, but still crisp. Reheat wok, and add additional peanut oil. When oil is hot, add meat with marinade. Allow to simmer 1 minute, then stir. Add broccoli and red pepper. Remove vegetables from pan when just cooked, but still crisp. Reheat wok, and add additional peanut oil. When oil is hot, add meat with marinade. Allow to simmer 1 minute, then stir. Add vegetables back to wok and toss. Drizzle a little sesame oil over pork and vegetables for flavor.

PLUM SAUCE MARINADE

---

1 tablespoon plum sauce
2 tablespoons dry sherry
1 tablespoon oyster sauce
1 tablespoon shoyu
1 teaspoon sugar
2 teaspoons cornstarch
2 cloves garlic, minced
1 small piece ginger root, minced

Combine all ingredients and mix well.

KIM GONSALVES
Executive Chef Culinary Shop
Honolulu, Hawaii

PORK TENDERLOIN
WITH AU GRATIN OF APPLES AND WILD RICE

Matthew created the Au Gratin of Apples for Ron, and it became one of his favorites to serve guests. When slicing pork tenderloin save the end pieces and use in a stir fry dish.

---

3 pork tenderloins
flour
5 tablespoons butter or margarine
2 cloves garlic, minced
pinch of ground nutmeg
pinch of ground ginger
salt and pepper
1/4 cup tawny port
1/3 cup apple brandy

---

serves 8

Slice pork tenderloins into 1 inch thick medallions from the center of the loin. Flour the pork medallions. In a large sauté pan over high heat, melt the butter. Sauté the garlic briefly, then add the floured pork medallions. Season to taste with spices and sauté 2 to 3 minutes each side.

Pour in port and apple brandy, flame and continue cooking until a sauce develops.

The sauce should be just thick enough to cling to the pork medallions. If the sauce is too thick, add a touch more apple brandy or white wine. Turn medallions in the sauce to coat both sides, then serve immediately with the Au Gratin of Apples and Wild Rice. Pour the remaining sauce over the medallions or serve in a gravy boat.

AU GRATIN OF APPLES

½ pound bacon, chopped
1 teaspoon minced garlic
4 tablespoons butter or margarine
1 large Vidalia or Walla Walla onion, slivered lengthwise
4 McIntosh apples, cored, peeled, sliced into 16 pieces, lengthwise
¼ teaspoon cinnamon
salt and pepper

In a large sauté pan over medium high heat, sauté the bacon halfway. Drain half the fat, then add the butter, garlic and onions. Cook until the bacon is thoroughly cooked, but not crispy, and the onions are almost browned. Add apples, cinnamon, salt and pepper. Warm through. Sprinkle with flour to lightly coat the apples. Turn the heat to high, pour in apple brandy and flame. Reduce heat and add whipping cream. Stir until the sauce thickens. Serve immediately or remove from heat and place in a buttered casserole dish and reheat at 400 degrees for 20 minutes.

WILD RICE

8 ounces wild rice
4 tablespoons butter
3 cloves garlic, minced
½ cup minced carrots
½ cup minced onions
½ cup minced celery
2 bay leaves
½ teaspoon thyme
1 teaspoon basil
salt and pepper
½ cup cooking sherry
beef broth

Preheat oven to 325 degrees. Cook the rice according to package directions, reducing the time slightly by 10 minutes. Drain and refresh rice under cold water.

Melt butter over medium high heat, sauté garlic, carrots, onions, and celery for 5 minutes, stirring occasionally. Add the bay leaves, thyme, basil, and salt and pepper to taste. Pour in cooking sherry and reduce by one half.

In a casserole dish, add the drained rice, vegetable mixture and enough beef broth to just come to the top of the rice. Adjust salt and pepper, cover and cook for 45 to 50 minutes.

MATTHEW WESTON
Matthew's Creative Cuisine restaurant and catering
Toledo, Ohio

ROAST LOIN OF PORK STUFFED WITH FRUIT

---

3 pound roast loin of pork
2 teaspoons ground cinnamon
4 teaspoons ground allspice
1 teaspoon ground clove
2 teaspoons ground nutmeg
4 teaspoons ground coriander
1/3 pound dried figs
1/3 pound pitted prunes
1/3 pound dried apricots
1 cup quince jelly, melted
1/2 cup vodka
1 cup veal stock
salt and pepper

---

serves 6

Mix five spices together and pat over pork loin, wrap with plastic wrap and refrigerate overnight. Before cooking, wipe the five spices off the meat and "stuff" it by taking a sharpening steel and pushing it through the center of the loin creating a long tunnel. Then use the steel to push the dried fruit into the meat alternating between figs, prunes and apricots as you go.

Preheat oven to 350 degrees. Roast the pork on a rack in a Calphalon roasting pan, roughly 24 minutes per pound. About 15 minutes before the roast is done begin to baste it every 5 minutes with the melted quince jelly. Check the roast about 12 minutes early, it should register 160 degrees on a meat thermometer. Let the roast rest about 20 minutes before carving.

To prepare gravy, place roasting pan on top of the stove. Over high heat, deglaze the pan with the vodka. Then add veal stock and reduce until the gravy is the consistency of a light syrup. Check seasoning, add salt and pepper to taste.

Glen T. Senk
Williams-Sonoma
San Francisco, California

STUFFED PORK TENDERLOIN
WITH DRUNKEN CABBAGE

This recipe was created by Gene Quint for a Sonoma cookbook, A CULINARY VISIT TO HISTORIC SONOMA, published by the Sonoma League for Historic Preservation.

---

2 boned pork tenderloins (3/4 to 1 pound each)
1 cup pitted dates
zest of 2 oranges
zest of 1 lemon
6 cloves garlic
salt

---

serves 6

Preheat oven to 350 degrees.

Make a cavity the length of each tenderloin with the help of a wooden spoon handle. Combine the dates and the zests. Stuff each cavity with this mixture. Make a paste with the garlic and salt using a mortar and pestle. Spread the paste over the tenderloins. Place the meat in a roasting pan and roast about 40 minutes or until pork reaches 170 degrees.

DRUNKEN CABBAGE

---

1 small cabbage head, coarsely shredded
1 onion, chopped
5 juniper berries, crushed
2 ounces gin
salt and pepper

---

serves 6

Toss the cabbage and onion with the berries and gin. Season with salt and pepper. Place the mixture in a buttered 2 quart baking dish and marinate for 1 to 2 hours.

Preheat oven to 350 degrees. Cover the dish and cook for about 45 minutes. Stir occasionally to keep the surface from drying out. The cabbage should still be moist and somewhat crisp when removed from the oven for serving.

Gene Quint
Sign of the Bear restaurant
Sonoma, California

CARIBBEAN CHICKEN

It is amazing how one can use the senses to differentiate various ethnic dishes. For instance, at the Epcot Center, if you close your eyes you know immediately where you are by the music, and the smells of the various dishes. We can do this at home by introducing our families to different ethnic dishes. This chicken dish will acquaint your family with Caribbean tastes. Pineapples can be substituted for mangos if desired.

---

6 chicken breast halves, boned, skinned
juice of 2 limes
3/4 cup white rum
1/4 cup light soy sauce
2 large cloves garlic, finely minced
grated fresh ginger (optional)
4 tablespoons butter
2 large onions, thinly sliced
4 to 6 large cloves garlic, sliced paper thin
1 green bell pepper, sliced thin
1 sweet red bell pepper, sliced thin
1 to 2 ripe mangoes peeled, sliced
1 cup chicken broth
salt and freshly ground pepper

---

serves 6

Rinse chicken and pat dry. Place in bowl, add lime juice and toss thoroughly. Combine rum, soy sauce, minced garlic and ginger for marinade. Pour marinade over chicken, coat thoroughly. Cover bowl and chill about 5 hours. Drain chicken and reserve marinade.

Preheat oven to 375 degrees. Melt butter in 5 quart sauté pan and brown chicken. Transfer to a plate and reserve. Sauté onions and garlic slices until onions are translucent, adding butter if needed. Stir in green and red pepper slices and sauté 2 to 3 minutes.

Return chicken to pan. Add mango slices, reserved marinade and chicken broth. Season with salt and pepper. Cover and bake in oven for 55 to 60 minutes.

Sonia R. Perez
The Kitchen Shop Inc.
Miami Lakes, Florida

pictured
roast chicken with garlic & new potatoes, 110
pork tenderloin with broccoli in plum sauce, 87
stuffed breast of capon allison, 112

CHICKEN BREAST PECAN

In the mid 70's Calphalon was gaining interest among cooking enthusiasts through the efforts of many specialty shops. One of these was the Cookshop, which Carole Kotkin owned at that time. In her role as a food consultant, Carole created this recipe for the Cook's Tour sponsored by Burdine's department store in Miami, Florida.

---

4 chicken breast halves, boned, skinned
1 cup flour
1 teaspoon salt
½ teaspoon freshly ground black pepper
2 egg whites, beaten until frothy
6 tablespoons Creole mustard or grainy Pommery mustard
1 cup finely ground pecans
1 cup fresh bread crumbs
2 tablespoons unsalted butter
2 tablespoons vegetable oil
½ cup heavy cream
pepper

---

serves 4

Combine flour, salt and pepper in a shallow bowl. Blend egg whites and 4 tablespoons of the mustard in a second bowl. Combine the pecans and bread crumbs in a third bowl. One at a time, dredge each chicken breast in the flour and shake off excess. Next, dip in the egg white mixture to coat. Finally, dip into the pecan/crumb mixture, pressing so the coating adheres to both sides. Place on a rack and refrigerate.

Heat the butter and oil over moderately high heat in a 12 inch omelette pan. When the foam subsides, cook chicken breasts on one side until crisp and brown, about 3 minutes. Turn, reduce the heat to moderately low and cook until the chicken has just lost its pinkness inside, about 5 minutes.

Meanwhile, in a 1½ quart sauce pan, warm the cream over moderate heat. Stir in the remaining mustard and season with pepper. Cook until warmed through, about 3 to 5 minutes. Slice the breasts on the diagonal and fan out decoratively on warmed serving plates. Pour sauce around chicken.

CAROLE KOTKIN
Food Consultant
Member of International Association of Culinary Professionals
Miami, Florida

CHICKEN & DUMPLINGS

This family favorite has soothed many common colds and warmed-up many rainy Sunday evenings over the years. Traditionally a French Acadia stew, this dish was brought to the family by a dear friend, Harriet Sims. Cook the chicken in stock for more flavor. Ron preferred the dish with the chicken pieces left whole rather than boned.

---

3 to 4 pound chicken, skinned, fat removed
2 onions with skins, cut into 1 inch pieces
3 carrots, cut into 1 inch pieces
3 celery stalks, cut into 1 inch pieces
2 to 3 sprigs of parsley
1 bay leaf
6 peppercorns
3 cloves
pinch of nutmeg
1 slice ginger root (optional)
2 teaspoons salt

---

serves 4

Combine ingredients in an 8 quart Calphalon stock pot. Add just enough water to cover chicken and vegetables, and bring to a slow boil. Reduce heat and simmer covered, about 2 hours. Remove foam from top as chicken cooks. Strain, returning liquid and boned chicken to the pot.

DUMPLINGS

---

1 cup flour plus additional as needed
pinch of baking powder
pinch of salt
½ cup cold water

Mix dry ingredients with water to make a soft dough. Turn out onto a well floured surface and knead a few times. Roll out thinly, like pasta, and cut into 1 inch squares. Bring broth to slow boil and add dumplings while it is boiling. Simmer until done, dumplings should puff a bit and be somewhat firm.

Becky Kasperzak
Perrysburg, Ohio

CHICKEN FAJITAS

Children love the activity of choosing their own ingredients and rolling them up in a tortilla. Vary the fajita fillings by substituting or adding different vegetables, meats or seafood to the ingredients.

---

6 chicken breast halves, boned, skinned
⅔ cup olive oil
⅔ cup picanté sauce
1½ teaspoons Creole seasonings or any meat seasoning
2 teaspoons lemon juice
2 teaspoons minced garlic
2 teaspoons Worcestershire sauce
flour tortilla shells
lettuce, chopped
tomato, chopped
avocado dip
sour cream
grated cheddar cheese
picanté sauce

---

serves 6

Place chicken breasts in 9x13 inch bake pan. Combine olive oil, picanté sauce, seasonings, lemon juice, garlic and Worcestershire sauce for a marinade. Pour marinade over chicken and coat thoroughly. Marinate overnight or at least 3 hours.

Grill chicken on barbeque. When done, slice against grain into strips. Serve on soft flour tortilla shells accompanied by lettuce, tomato, avocado dip, sour cream, grated cheddar cheese and picanté sauce.

Bonnie Aronson
J. Aronson, Ltd.
New Orleans, Louisiana

CHICKEN LOAF
WITH FRESH MUSHROOM SAUCE

2⅔ cups chicken stock
2 cups cubed day old bread
3½ cups cooked chicken, cubed
1½ cups cooked brown rice
4 eggs, beaten
¼ cup finely chopped green bell pepper
¼ cup finely chopped red bell pepper
½ teaspoon salt
2 teaspoons minced fresh sage or 1 teaspoon dried
2 teaspoons minced fresh rosemary or 1 teaspoon dried
¼ teaspoon black pepper
1 small onion, finely chopped

serves 4-6

Preheat oven to 350 degrees. Pour chicken stock over bread cubes, let stand 5 minutes. In a separate bowl, combine chicken with remaining ingredients, stirring well. Add chicken mixture to bread cubes, stir until blended. Spoon mixture into a well buttered Calphalon loaf pan, then place loaf pan in a shallow baking dish with 1 inch of water. Bake for 1 hour. Cool for 30 minutes, invert onto serving platter. Serve with Mushroom Sauce.

MUSHROOM SAUCE

⅛ cup unsalted butter
⅛ cup plus 1 tablespoon flour
1¼ cups chicken stock
¾ cup sliced fresh mushrooms
1 tablespoon chopped fresh parsley
½ teaspoon lemon juice
½ teaspoon paprika

Melt butter in a small sauce pan over low heat. Gradually add flour, stirring until smooth. Cook 1 minute, stirring constantly. Stir in stock a little at a time over medium heat until sauce is thick and bubbly. Remove from heat and stir in remaining ingredients. Double the sauce if desired.

Bev and John Shaffer
What's Cooking?, Inc.
Akron, Ohio

CHICKEN MARSALA

1 pound chicken breasts, boned, skinned
flour
salt and pepper
2 tablespoons olive oil
3 cloves garlic, chopped
1 cup sweet marsala wine
½ cup tomato sauce
1 teaspoon oregano
salt and pepper

serves 4

Slice chicken breasts into thin pieces. Pat dry. Dredge each piece in flour seasoned with salt and pepper. Heat olive oil in a sauté pan, on medium high heat. Sauté chopped garlic in oil. Add chicken pieces and quickly sauté until browned, removing chicken from pan as pieces are cooked. Deglaze pan with wine, then reduce heat to medium. Cook 2 to 3 minutes to remove alcohol. Stir in tomato sauce and oregano. Season to taste with salt and pepper. Cook 2 to 3 minutes until mixture bubbles. Return chicken to pan and cook for 4 minutes. Serve over buttered pasta. Sprinkle with freshly grated Parmesan cheese.

Glenn Cunningham
Lechmere
Boston, Massachusetts

CORNISH HEN SUPREME

3 Rock Cornish hens, halved
½ cup barbecue sauce
2 tablespoons soy sauce
13 ounces Chambord apricot preserves
8 ounces sliced water chestnuts
onion, thinly sliced
1 small red bell pepper, julienned
1 small green bell pepper, julienned

serves 3

Preheat oven to 400 degrees.

Wash and dry hens. Put hens skin side up in roasting pan. Mix together barbecue sauce, soy sauce and preserves. Pour sauce over hens. Bake for 30 minutes.

Add water chestnuts and onions. Reduce heat to 350 degrees and bake for another 30 minutes. Add red and green peppers and bake for another 20 minutes. Serve over rice.

Arlene Harris
Chef's Catalog
Northbrook, Illinois

CUBAN CHICKEN

Add a plain green salad and this chicken dish is perfect for family meals or for unexpected guests.

---

2 fryer (or broiler) chickens, cut up
5 cloves garlic, minced
1 large yellow onion, chopped
½ green bell pepper, chopped
30 ounces canned tomatoes (crushed or whole cut up)
4 bay leaves
1 teaspoon cumin seed
1½ teaspoon dried oregano
1 cup raisins
1 cup stuffed green olives
3 tablespoons olive oil
3 tablespoons red wine vinegar

---

serves 6

Place chickens (skinned or unskinned) in a large deep sauce pan. Add garlic, onion, green pepper, tomatoes, bay leaves, cumin, oregano, raisins, olives, oil and vinegar.

Cover and bring to boil. Reduce heat to low and simmer for 1 hour, turning chicken occasionally. Remove chicken to a platter and serve with the sauce over rice or noodles.

Madelin and David Wexler
Cahners Publishing Company
David is a Board Member of the American Institute of Wine and Food
Des Plaines, Illinois

GRILLED CITRUS CHICKEN

6 chicken breast halves, boned
2 to 3 cloves garlic, minced
salt and pepper
½ cup brown sugar
3 tablespoons grainy mustard
¼ cup vinegar
juice of 1 to 2 limes
juice of 1 large lemon
6 tablespoons mild olive oil or vegetable oil

serves 6

Mince garlic in a food processor. Add salt, pepper, sugar, mustard, vinegar, lime and lemon juice to food processor. Blend with steel blade. Slowly add oil through feed tube while machine is running.

Place chicken breasts in a large zip lock, heavy duty, plastic bag and add marinade. Coat chicken thoroughly. Refrigerate overnight, turning the bag several times to marinate evenly. Bring to room temperature 1 hour before grilling.

Grill chicken breasts on charcoal grill, 4 minutes on each side. Garnish with lemon and lime slices and fresh herbs.

Linda Zey Davis
Member of the International Association of Culinary Professionals
Kansas City, Missouri

HOT CHICKEN SALAD

Freeze half or all of this hot chicken salad to use at a later date. Served with a croissant and a tossed green salad this is a good choice for a special luncheon. Leftover turkey can be used in place of chicken.

---

4 chicken breast halves, cooked, boned, skinned
1 cup mayonnaise
1 cup sour cream
3 hard boiled eggs, chopped
5½ ounces cream of chicken soup
2 cups finely chopped celery
8 ounces sliced water chestnuts, drained
4 ounces mushroom pieces, drained
½ cup slivered almonds
2 tablespoons minced onions
2 tablespoons lemon juice
1 teaspoon salt
¼ teaspoon black pepper
1 cup grated cheddar cheese
3½ ounce can onion rings

---

serves 6

Preheat oven to 350 degrees.

Cut chicken into 1 inch pieces. In a large bowl blend mayonnaise and sour cream. Add the chicken pieces and remaining ingredients, except cheese and onion rings.

Mix together, then pour into a 13 inch au gratin pan and sprinkle with cheese. Bake uncovered for 30 minutes. Remove from oven, sprinkle onion rings on top and bake for another 15 minutes.

Leandra Walker
Gourmet Galley
Paducah, Kentucky

HUNGARIAN CHICKEN

---

3 to 4 pound fryer chicken
garlic powder
paprika
pepper
2 tablespoons oil
2 red bell peppers, chopped
2 large onions, chopped
1 pound mushrooms, sliced
1 cup white wine
28 ounce can chopped tomatoes, drained
6 ounces tomato paste
1 tablespoon sugar (optional)
1 cup sour cream

---

serves 4-6

Preheat oven to 350 degrees.

Cut chicken into serving pieces and season with garlic powder, paprika and pepper. Bake for 40 minutes.

Heat oil in a 5 quart sauté pan. Sauté peppers and onions until onions are translucent. Add mushrooms, sauté for a minute. Add the wine, tomatoes, tomato paste and sugar and stir until mixed. Add sour cream and stir through tomato mixture. Place cooked chicken in mixture, cover and simmer for 10 minutes. Serve over noodles or rice.

Denise Madden
The Kellen Company
Drexel Hill, Pennsylvania

PETTO DI POLLO IN LATTUGA

CHICKEN BREASTS WRAPPED IN LETTUCE

5 medium size chicken breast halves, boned, skinned
4 romaine lettuce leaves
3 cups half and half
1 egg yolk
pinch of nutmeg
salt and pepper
1 cup chicken broth
1 cup butter
1 cup port wine
1 tablespoon minced shallots

serves 4

Preheat oven to 350 degrees. Butter a baking pan.

Puree 1 breast of chicken in a food processor or blender until smooth, about 1½ minutes. Steam romaine lettuce leaves quickly and refresh under cold water. Reserve.

Mix half and half, egg yolk and nutmeg. Set aside while preparing the chicken breast.

Pound remaining 4 chicken breasts to about ½ inch thick for stuffing. Season with salt and pepper. Lay breast flat, spread one-fourth of the chicken puree in center of each and roll.

Wrap each breast carefully in refreshed lettuce leaf, folding when necessary. Place lettuce wrapped chicken in a buttered baking pan, pour chicken broth over breasts and dot with butter. Cover and bake for 20 minutes.

Meanwhile, in a small sauce pan mix port and shallots. Reduce over medium heat for 3 minutes, then slowly stir in half and half mixture. Season with salt and pepper.

When chicken is cooked through, place each portion on individual plates. Strain the port sauce. Pour one-fourth of the sauce over each portion.

PIERO SELVAGGIO
Valentino's restaurant
Santa Monica, California

POULET FRANCOISE

Roast chicken always tastes good and cooking it with wine and herbs makes it extra special for guests. Frances said she created this recipe to take advantage of the even heat distribution of the Calphalon roasting pan. She serves the chicken at the table in the roast pan.

---

1 whole chicken
6 tablespoons butter or margarine
3 to 4 cloves garlic or
2 cloves elephant garlic
2 to 3 tablespoons Italian herbs
salt and freshly ground pepper
¼ cup white wine
8 ounces mushrooms, sliced
2 tablespoons potato flour or cornstarch
½ cup chicken broth

---

serves 4-6

Preheat oven to 400 degrees.

Butter a Calphalon 14 inch roasting pan with 2 tablespoons butter. Place garlic in bottom of pan.

Cut backbone off chicken, flatten and cut up either side of breastbone. Lay flattened chicken over garlic, skin side up. Melt 2 tablespoons butter with Italian herbs and brush on chicken. Season with salt and pepper. Roast in oven for 1 hour to 1 hour and 10 minutes, adding wine after 30 minutes.

While chicken is cooking, sauté mushrooms in remaining 2 tablespoons butter. Set aside and add potato flour.

Remove chicken to cutting board, add broth to roast pan and mash garlic. Place pan on stove and heat to simmer. Add mushrooms and stir until sauce is thickened. Cut chicken into pieces and add to roast pan. Serve with pasta, rice or noodles.

Frances Enslein
Frances Enslein Cooking School
Greenwich, Connecticut

RED HOT CHICKEN ENCHILADAS

4 large chicken breast halves
2 carrots, diced
2 onions, chopped
salt and pepper
3 tablespoons oil
2 medium onions, chopped
2 red bell peppers, cut into 1 inch slices
1 teaspoon ground black pepper
½ teaspoon cayenne pepper
¼ teaspoon salt
2¼ cups Monterey Jack cheese, grated
8 8-inch flour tortillas
Red Hot Sauce

serves 4-8

Combine chicken, carrots, onions, salt and pepper in an 8 quart Calphalon stock pot. Add water to cover and bring to a boil. Simmer 20 minutes. Remove chicken, cool, discard skin and bones and shred into 1 inch pieces.

In a sauté pan heat 2 tablespoons of oil. Sauté onion for 1 minute, then add shredded chicken, red peppers, black and cayenne pepper, and salt. Sauté for 5 minutes, remove from pan, and set aside.

Preheat oven to 350 degrees. Spread a thin layer of Red Hot Sauce in an 8x13 inch bake pan. Heat 1 tablespoon of oil in a 10″ omelette pan, then heat each tortilla for 15 seconds on both sides. Spread ½ cup filling and ¼ cup cheese on each tortilla and roll up. Place tortillas in bake pan. Pour sauce over tortillas and sprinkle with cheese. Cover with foil and bake for 30 minutes.

RED HOT SAUCE

2 ½ cups diced, canned tomatoes with green chilies
¾ cup tomato paste
1 teaspoon ground black pepper
½ teaspoon cayenne pepper
½ cup cilantro, chopped, lightly packed

Combine ingredients in a sauce pan, and simmer for 20 to 30 minutes.

Paul Angelo LoGiudice
Culinary Events Specialist
Commercial Aluminum Cookware Company

ROAST CHICKEN
WITH GARLIC AND NEW POTATOES

A meal to serve to family or friends, it can easily be doubled or tripled. Be sure to leave garlic skins on when baking because the clove of garlic will steam in its skin and become very soft and spreadable for delicious garlic bread. Finish this comforting dinner with some pears, cheese and a glass of port.

---

3 pound whole chicken
salt and freshly ground pepper
1 large garlic head, cloves separated but not peeled
4 bay leaves
1½ teaspoons dried rosemary, crumbled
¼ cup olive oil
6 2-inch diameter red new potatoes, halved
½ large lemon

---

serves 2

Preheat oven to 375 degrees.

Season chicken cavity with salt and pepper. Halve 2 garlic cloves and place in cavity with 2 bay leaves. Tie chicken legs together to hold shape, tuck wings under. Rub rosemary into chicken. Season with salt and pepper.

Heat oil in heavy, large, ovenproof sauté pan over high heat. Add remaining garlic cloves and stir 30 seconds. Add chicken, potatoes and remaining 2 bay leaves. Season potatoes with salt and pepper. Brown chicken on all sides. Squeeze lemon over chicken and potatoes. Transfer pan to oven. Baste occasionally. Roast until juices run clear when chicken is pierced in thickest part of thigh, about 1 hour. Transfer chicken, garlic and potatoes to platter. Degrease juices, if desired. Carve chicken and spoon pan juices over. Serve with garlic, potatoes and French bread, spreading the garlic on the bread.

William J. Garry
Editor-in-Chief, BON APPÉTIT magazine
Member of the International Association of Culinary Professionals
New York, New York

SAUTERNE CHICKEN CURRY

6 chicken breast halves, boned, skinned
½ cup vegetable oil
½ teaspoon salt
½ teaspoon white pepper
1 teaspoon curry powder
½ teaspoon chili powder
½ cup water
½ cup Sauterne wine
1 cup finely chopped onion
3 large garlic cloves, minced
1 tablespoon chicken bouillon granules
1 cup rice
1 tablespoon flour
2 tablespoons water
1 cup whipping cream

serves 6

Preheat oven to 325 degrees.

In a large casserole or Dutch oven, brown chicken in oil. While browning, combine salt, pepper, curry powder and chili powder. When chicken is golden brown, combine water and wine, then pour over chicken. Sprinkle chicken with combined seasonings. Add the onion, garlic and chicken bouillon to the casserole. Place in oven and cook for 30 minutes or until chicken is done.

While chicken is cooking, prepare rice according to directions. Spread cooked rice on an ovenproof platter. Arrange chicken breasts on the rice and place in oven. Adjust temperature to keep the platter warm.

Make a thin paste with flour and water. Place casserole pan on stove and simmer over low heat. Add flour paste to drippings, stirring constantly, until paste is completely mixed in and smooth. Slowly pour in whipping cream and continue to stir until the sauce is smooth and heated through. Adjust seasonings. Pour the sauce over the bed of rice and chicken. Garnish the platter with parsley sprigs and cherry tomatoes.

Geneva Williams
Gourmet Curiosities, Etc.
Member of the International Association of Culinary Professionals
Sylvania, Ohio

STUFFED BREAST OF CAPON ALLISON

---

2 fresh capons
1¼ cup heavy whipping cream
3 egg whites
2 tablespoons cognac or fine brandy
nutmeg
salt and pepper
6 tablespoons roasted pine nuts or pistachios
4 quarts chicken stock
4 tablespoons unsalted butter
3 leaves fresh basil, chopped

---

serves 4

Disjoint each capon into skinless breasts, legs and thighs. Set breasts aside. Trim meat off legs and thighs and dice into tiny pieces. Place meat pieces in food processor and puree for 1 minute. Blend in 1 cup cream, egg whites and cognac. Season to taste with nutmeg and salt and pepper. Place mixture in mixing bowl, add roasted pine nuts. Set aside in refrigerator.

Place capon breast flat on work surface. With a thin, very sharp knife, slit a pocket into breast starting at top, being careful not to puncture sides. Fill a pastry bag with capon mixture and stuff each capon breast until full. Wrap each breast in cheesecloth, tie with string for poaching.

Place each breast in simmering chicken stock for 15 minutes or until firm. Remove and let rest for 10 minutes.

Pour 4 cups chicken stock into a small sauce pan and reduce by half. Stir in ¼ cup cream and reduce until sauce slightly thickens. Stir butter into sauce along with chopped fresh basil.

Remove cloth from breast and slice on a bias widthwise across breast, and fan onto plate. Spoon sauce over the top. Serve with fresh linguine or fettuccine.

Bennett Mulé
Executive Chef, Onwentsia Club
Lake Forest, Illinois

POLENTA E RAGÙ DI SELVAGGINA

POLENTA WITH WILD GAME

---

3 quails, boned, halved
2 pigeons, boned, cut into four pieces
4 rabbit legs, halved
½ cup olive oil
½ onion, julienned
1 carrot, julienned
2 celery stalks, julienned
1 teaspoon chopped fresh thyme
1 teaspoon chopped fresh sage
1 gallon red wine
1 quart brown stock
1 cup chicken broth
4 ounces fresh porcini or shitake mushrooms
¼ cup butter plus 2 teaspoons
1½ cups instant polenta
salt and pepper

---

serves 6

Heat olive oil in a deep frying pan. Add julienned vegetables and brown. Add meats and sauté until they begin to color. Add thyme and sage, then slowly pour in wine. When color darkens, add brown stock and chicken broth. Cover and simmer for 20 minutes. Add mushrooms and simmer for 10 minutes. Season with salt and pepper.

Five minutes before serving, prepare polenta by bringing 1½ quarts of water to a boil. Add 2 teaspoons butter, then stir in polenta with a wooden spoon. Stir for about 5 minutes. Just before serving add ¼ cup of butter for extra flavor.

Place a serving of polenta on each plate with a piece of quail, pigeon and rabbit. Spoon sauce over meat.

PIERO SELVAGGIO
Valentino's restaurant
Santa Monica, California

LASAGNA OF QUAIL, FOIE GRAS & WILD MUSHROOMS

The beautiful presentation of this dish, as drawn by Charlie Trotter, illustrates how the visual arrangement of food is as important to the dining process as the preparation.

---

4 quail, completely boned, except for leg bones
1½ pounds assorted wild mushrooms (whatever is in season)
1 pear
½ cup cubed bacon
1 carrot, peeled, chopped
1 onion, chopped
1 celery stalk, chopped
2 cups red wine
1½ quarts duck stock
2 sprigs fresh thyme
salt and pepper
hazelnut oil
butter
½ pound foie gras, cut into eight 1 ounce slices
16 2x3 inch pieces of spinach or wild mushroom pasta
1½ tablespoons chopped chives

---

serves 4

Cut each quail into 8 pieces and reserve. Clean and thinly slice half of the mushrooms, chop the other half into bite size pieces. Set mushrooms aside. Using a petite melon baller, cut out 32 pear balls, preferably with a little skin on each one, set aside. Save remainder of pear.

In a 5 quart sauté pan, render fat from the bacon, then evenly brown carrots, onions and celery. Deglaze pan with red wine and reduce to a half cup. Chop remainder of pear and add to vegetable mixture. Pour in duck stock and reduce to 1 cup, skimming fat along the way. Add thyme during last minutes of cooking, strain, season with salt and pepper. Reserve.

In a small amount of hazelnut oil, sauté all the quail pieces over medium high heat until medium rare, about 1½ to 2 minutes. Remove quail from pan, and keep warm. Simultaneously, sauté the mushrooms in butter, in two separate pans, the sliced in one and the chopped in another. Remove mushrooms from their pans and keep warm.

Sauté foie gras pieces in a large, fairly hot pan, 4 pieces at a time. Drain the fat continuously so that the foie gras can attain a crispiness. When all pieces are cooked, reserve and keep warm. Finally, cook pasta sheets in boiling, salted water to al dente, drain, and toss with a tablespoon of hazelnut oil.

On 4 plates place a small amount of sautéed, sliced mushrooms, top with 2 slices of the boneless quail. Then place a pasta sheet and a foie gras slice. Place another pasta, then more sliced mushrooms and 2 quail pieces, then pasta, and distribute the remaining foie gras. Top the "lasagna" with the last piece of pasta. Place the chopped mushroom pieces, the quail leg pieces and the pear balls around the "lasagna." Sprinkle with chives and pour the sauce around the edge of the plate.

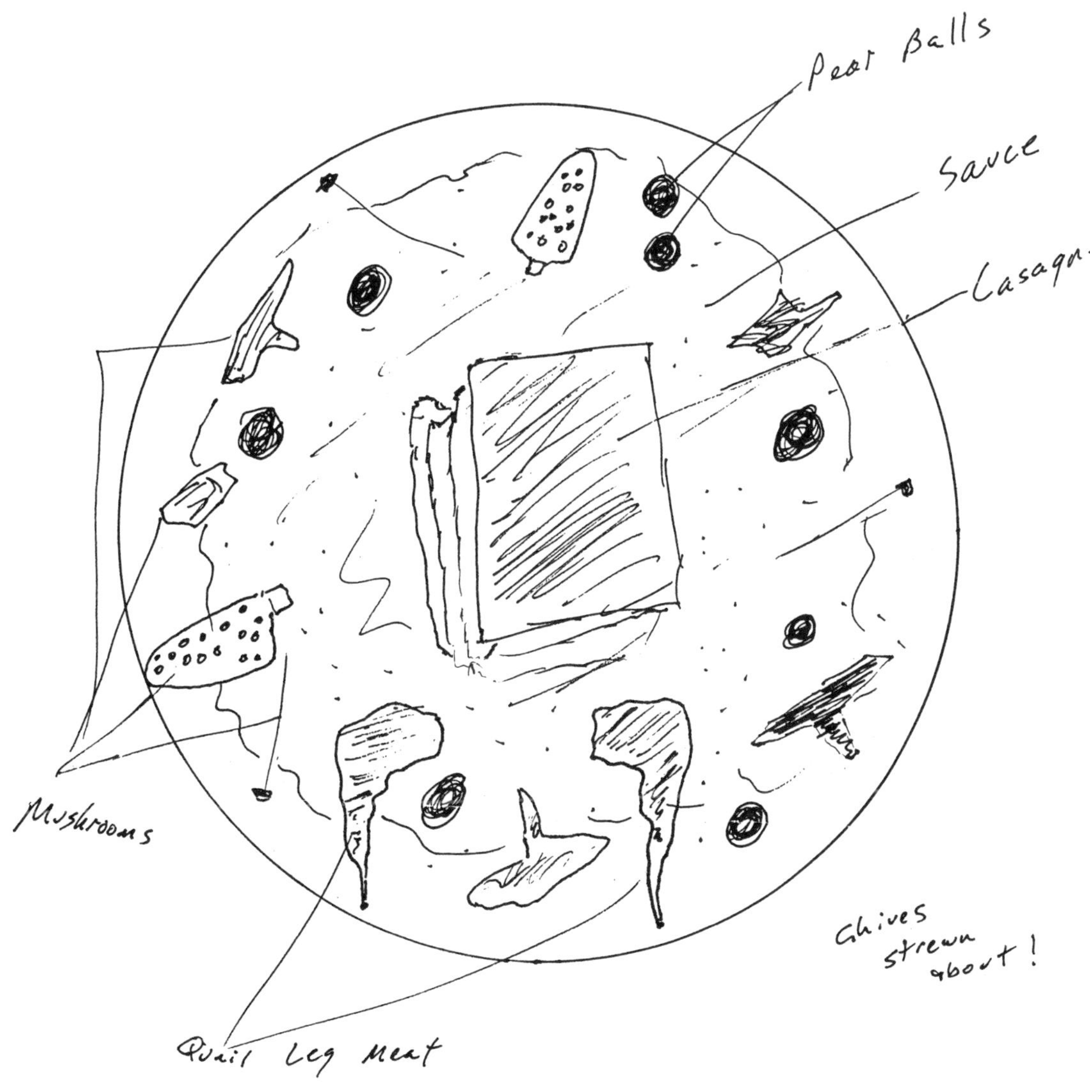

Charlie Trotter
Charlie Trotter's restaurant
Chicago, Illinois

SAUTÉED QUAIL
WITH HERB POLENTA STUFFING

Paul created this dish for a Calphalon Thanksgiving Day seminar and served it with Sweet Potato Pancakes. Polenta, which is a mush made from cornmeal, is native to Northern Italy. It can be made a day in advance, cooled to firm, then cut into shapes and sautéed. Try it as a substitute for rice, potatoes or pasta.

---

8 quail
black pepper
1 tablespoon flour
3 tablespoons butter
½ cup Cognac
¼ cup shallots
1 cup chicken stock

---

serves 4

With a pair of poultry shears, cut the backbone from each quail, flatten out and sprinkle generously with pepper.

Make a beurre manié (kneaded butter) by blending flour and 1 tablespoon of butter into a smooth paste. Set aside.

Preheat a Calphalon 3 quart sauté pan on medium heat. Add 2 tablespoons of butter. When butter is bubbling briskly, place 4 quails into pan, breast side down. Sear, then turn and sear other sides. Return quails to breast side and cook 8 to 10 minutes. Turn, and cook other sides an additional 8 minutes. Remove quails to platter and keep warm in oven. Repeat with remaining quails.

Deglaze pan with Cognac, using the flat edge of a metal spatula to release drippings from pan bottom. Reduce heat and add shallots. Cook for 4 to 5 minutes. Pour in chicken stock and bring to a boil. Whisk in beurre manié and allow sauce to thicken. Pour sauce over quail. Serve with Herb Polenta Stuffing.

HERB POLENTA STUFFING

8 cups chicken stock
1 teaspoon rosemary
½ teaspoon thyme
½ teaspoon sage
¼ teaspoon black pepper
2 cups yellow cornmeal
2 tablespoons butter
1 cup finely chopped celery
1 white onion, finely chopped
1 cup finely chopped mushrooms
salt and pepper
2 tablespoons olive oil

Bring 2 quarts of chicken stock to boil in a 4½ quart sauce pan. Add rosemary, thyme, sage and pepper. While whisking vigorously, slowly pour in cornmeal, making sure there are no lumps. Reduce to low heat and cook for 45 minutes, stirring occasionally.

Preheat a 10 inch omelette pan on medium heat. When pan is hot, add 2 tablespoons of butter. Sauté celery, onions and mushrooms until onions are translucent. Drain off excess liquid and reserve.

Fold the vegetables into the cooked polenta. Season to taste with salt and pepper.

Butter a cookie sheet and spread polenta to ¾ inch thick. Cool, then cover and refrigerate for 2 hours or overnight. Cut into 2 inch triangles. Preheat a 3 quart sauté pan. Heat 2 tablespoons of olive oil, then add polenta triangles. Cook on each side for 2 to 3 minutes until golden brown.

Paul Angelo LoGuidice
Culinary Events Specialist
Commercial Aluminum Cookware Company

SUPREME OF ILLINOIS PHEASANT
WITH CHANTERELLES

---

1 rooster pheasant
kosher salt
white pepper
2 tablespoons corn oil
1 tablespoon finely minced shallot
1 small celery root (celeriac) peeled, cut into fine slivers
12 medium chanterelles, left whole
1/4 cup dry sherry
2 teaspoons soy sauce
1/2 cup Natural Pheasant Jus
3/4 cup Autumn Vegetable Salpicon

---

serves 2

Remove the breasts from a rooster pheasant leaving the skin on, and the wing bones attached. Cut the skin and meat away from the wing bones and set aside with the pheasant bones and legs. Season the breasts with salt and pepper, then refrigerate while the Natural Pheasant Jus is cooking.

Bring pheasant breasts to room temperature. Preheat oven to 375 degrees.

Heat corn oil in a deep sauté pan over medium heat. Place pheasant breasts skin side down and brown. Once the skin is brown, remove the breasts and sauté shallots, celeriac and chanterelles for 30 seconds. Pour in sherry, soy and Natural Pheasant Jus. Bring to a simmer and return pheasant breasts, skin side up. Put in oven and bake for 7 to 9 minutes.

Remove the breasts, slice and arrange on top of a nest of celeriac. Arrange the chanterelles and Autumn Vegetable Salpicon around the nest and spoon Jus over all.

NATURAL PHEASANT JUS

pheasant bones, legs, and wing trimmings
bay leaf
thyme
peppercorns
trimmings from vegetables
trimmings from mushrooms
white wine
consommé

Place bones and legs in a stock pot with bay leaf, thyme, peppercorns and trimmings from the vegetables and mushrooms. Pour in white wine and consommé, just covering the bones. Simmer 2 hours and strain. Freeze the remaining Natural Pheasant Jus.

AUTUMN VEGETABLE SALPICON

1 ear fresh corn kernels
French green beans
red bell pepper
chanterelles
1 teaspoon minced garlic
1 teaspoon fresh minced tarragon
dash of sherry
2 tablespoons corn oil
kosher salt
ground white pepper
2 tablespoons butter

Cut corn kernels from cob. Cut an equal amount of French beans, red pepper and chanterelles, uniformly to the same size and amount as the corn kernels.

Place the vegetables in a bowl and mix with garlic, tarragon, sherry, corn oil, and salt and pepper to taste. Heat a medium size sauté pan, add butter and when lightly brown add vegetable mixture. Cook 2 to 3 minutes, serve as garnish with pheasant.

CHEF CLIFFORD PLEAU
Le Ciel Bleu restaurant
The Mayfair Regent
Chicago, Illinois

WILD GAME DEMI-GLACE & BRAISED RABBIT LEGS

Demi-glace is the base of all new game sauces and soups.

$2\frac{1}{2}$ pounds veal bones
2 duck carcasses
2 leeks, sliced
3 onions, quartered
4 carrots, cut into 1 inch pieces
white wine
1 grouse
1 pheasant
1 wood pigeon
3 rabbit legs
3 celery stalks, cut into 1 inch pieces
6 cloves garlic
6 bay leaves
2 teaspoon dried thyme
1 teaspoon peppercorns
1 bunch parsley
1 bottle red wine
1 bottle port wine

Preheat oven to 450 degrees.

Place veal bones and duck carcasses in roasting pan and roast for 15 minutes. Add leeks, onions and carrots and roast until vegetables are brown. Transfer veal bones, duck carcasses, leeks, onions and carrots to 16 quart stock pot. Deglaze roasting pan with white wine and add pan contents to stock pot. Add remainder of ingredients, except red and port wines, to stock pot.

Fill stock pot with water and bring to a boil. Skim foam from surface. Reduce to a slow, barely perceptible simmer. Simmer 12 to 16 hours (overnight), always keeping solids just covered with water.

Strain liquid into an 8 quart sauce pan, discard bones and vegetables. Reduce liquid over high heat to 4 quarts. Add red and port wines. Reduce liquid to 1 quart. Place demi-glace in 1 cup containers and freeze.

BRAISED RABBIT LEGS

---

6 to 8 rabbit legs
olive oil
4 carrots, cut into 1 inch pieces
2 pints pearl onions, peeled
1 bottle red wine
1 cup Wild Game Demi-glace
8 cloves garlic, peeled
bay leaf
dried thyme
salt and pepper

---

serves 6-8

Heat oil in large sauce pan. Add carrots and pearl onions and cook until golden brown. Deglaze pan with red wine, and reduce by 25 percent. Add Wild Game Demi-glace. Bring to a boil on medium heat and add rabbit legs, garlic, bay leaf and dried thyme. Cover and reduce heat to simmer. Cook until rabbit legs are tender, about 30 minutes. If sauce reduces too much, add water. If sauce is too thin when rabbit legs are ready to serve, remove legs and vegetables and reduce sauce until syrupy. Season to taste. Serve over fettuccine.

George Faison
D'ARTAGNAN, Inc.
Board Member of the American Institute of Wine and Food
Jersey City, New Jersey

VENISON WITH JUNIPER & PORT SAUCE

This recipe was featured in the December, 1988 METROPOLITAN HOME as a Christmas Feast with Friends. Juniper berries are spice berries that have the aroma of a pine forest. They are used to flavor meats, sauces and stuffings, as well as wild game. Juniper berries are sold dried and can be found in the spice section of most supermarkets.

---

4 to 5 pound boneless leg of venison
salt and pepper
2 cloves garlic, mashed
2 teaspoons fresh savory or 1 teaspoon dried
½ cup Dijon mustard

---

serves 6

Preheat oven to 350 degrees.

Rub venison with salt, pepper, garlic and savory, then coat with mustard. Roast about 20 minutes per pound (use a meat thermometer, rare meat registers 125 degrees, medium 135 degrees). Let finished roast sit 15 minutes before carving.

JUNIPER AND PORT SAUCE

---

1 cup port
2 cups beef stock
10 crushed juniper berries
2 tablespoons butter, cut into small pieces
fresh currants or grapes

Deglaze roasting pan with port and transfer to sauce pan. Add beef stock and juniper berries. Cook over medium heat until sauce is reduced by half. Strain sauce to remove juniper berries and return to sauce pan.

Over medium heat, quickly whisk in butter one piece at a time, do not boil. The sauce will thicken slightly. Spoon sauce over sliced venison. Garnish with currants and grapes.

Donna Warner
Food and Design Editor, METROPOLITAN HOME magazine
New York, New York

PASTA, RICE & RISOTTO

FARFALLE CON ASPARAGI E PISELLI

PASTA WITH ASPARAGUS AND SNOW PEAS

4 tablespoons butter
2 cups heavy cream
4 tablespoons Parmesan cheese
salt and pepper
1 pound Spinach or Tomato Farfalle, or a combination
2 tablespoons olive oil
2 ounces asparagus, cut into ½ inch pieces
4 ounces snow peas, cleaned

serves 8

Combine butter and cream in a sauce pan. Reduce by 35 percent. Add cheese and season with salt and pepper. Simmer until cheese is dissolved. Cook pasta in boiling water until al dente, approximately 15 minutes. Drain and toss into cream sauce, making sure pasta is well coated.

Heat oil in sauté pan. Sauté asparagus and snow peas until vegetables are crisp and lightly browned. Place pasta on plates and garnish with vegetables.

SPINACH FARFALLE

1½ ounces frozen spinach
3 eggs
½ teaspoon salt
1½ to 2 cups flour

yields 1 pound pasta

Defrost spinach and squeeze out all excess water. Puree spinach in blender. In a mixing bowl, combine eggs, spinach and salt. Blend with a dough hook until well mixed. Slowly add flour to mixture until dough pulls away from the side of the bowl. Finish by hand, working in additional flour as needed, until dough is smooth and elastic. Let rest in refrigerator for 1 hour.

Using a pasta machine, roll the dough out on a thin setting. Lay dough on a floured pastry board and with a serrated, hand wheel cutter, cut 1x2 inch rectangles. Pinch each rectangle in the center to form a bow tie shape. Be sure that pasta maintains form.

TOMATO FARFALLE

3 eggs
2 tablespoons tomato paste
1½ teaspoons salt
1½ to 2 cups flour

yields 1 pound pasta

Break eggs into the bowl of a mixer. Add tomato paste and salt. Mix together. With a dough hook mix in half of the flour. Add remaining flour, a little at a time, until dough pulls away from the side of the bowl. Finish by hand, working in additional flour as needed, until dough is smooth and elastic. Let rest in refrigerator for 1 hour.

Using a pasta machine, roll the dough out on a thin setting. Lay dough on a floured pastry board and with a serrated, hand wheel cutter, cut 1x2 inch rectangles. Pinch each rectangle in the center to form a bow tie shape. Be sure that pasta maintains form.

Suzanne Schroeder
Spiaggia restaurant
Chicago, Illinois

LASAGNA AL PESTO

1 pound fresh spinach
1 cup minced onion
3 tablespoons olive oil
½ cup grated Parmesan cheese
Pesto Sauce
4 cups ricotta cheese
¼ pound sunflower seeds (optional)
freshly ground pepper
20 to 24 spinach lasagna noodles
1 pound mozzarella cheese, thin slices or grated

serves 6

Preheat oven to 350 degrees.

Clean spinach and chop fine in food processor or blender. Sauté onions in 2 tablespoons of olive oil, stir in chopped raw spinach with hot onions. Transfer to large bowl. Add Parmesan cheese, pesto sauce, ricotta cheese, sunflower seeds and pepper to taste. Mix thoroughly with spoon.

Cook pasta al dente, drain and drizzle with remaining olive oil. Layer in 9x13 inch bakepan starting with noodles, filling, mozzarella cheese and ending with noodles. Sprinkle with Parmesan cheese and drizzle with olive oil. Cover with foil and bake for 35 to 40 minutes.

PESTO SAUCE

1 cup fresh basil
2 small cloves garlic
½ cup walnuts
½ cup olive oil
½ cup fresh Parmesan cheese
salt and pepper

Put basil, garlic and walnuts in blender or food processor and chop. Leave motor running and add the olive oil in a slow, steady stream. Shut motor off, add Parmesan cheese, pinch of salt and a liberal grinding of pepper. Process briefly to combine ingredients. Scrape into bowl and cover until ready to use.

Sally Jo Mullen
Les Chefs D'Aspen
Member of the International Association of Culinary Professionals
Aspen, Colorado

LEFT BANK LASAGNA

Joann suggested using a frozen spinach soufflé, available at most supermarkets, if you are unable to find spinach terrine with Roquefort.

---

1 pound fresh lasagna noodles
2 cups mascarpone
16 ounces spinach terrine with Roquefort, cut in thin strips
1/2 cup red bell peppers, roasted, peeled, seeded, chopped
1/2 cup nicoise or ligurian olives, cut in half
1/2 cup chopped filberts
1/3 cup grated Romano cheese

---

serves 6

Oil an 8x13 inch baking pan. Cut fresh pasta into strips measuring 2 inches by 13 inches. Cook in boiling water for 2 minutes.

Preheat oven to 350 degrees.

Layer in pan: 4 strips pasta, 1 cup mascarpone and 8 ounces spinach terrine strips to make one layer. Sprinkle 1/4 cup pepper, 1/4 cup olives and 1/4 cup filberts over spinach terrine. Repeat procedure to create second layer, ending with filberts. Sprinkle with Romano cheese. Bake for 30 minutes. Cool for 15 minutes before cutting.

JOANN FORTUNE
The Eight Mice
Lafayette, Indiana

LINGUINE WITH CHICKEN

Many people love the flavor of garlic and this dish combines the taste and aroma in a light pasta sauce. Similar in spirit to linguine with clam sauce, this dish is perfect for children who don't appreciate the taste of clams.

---

2 chicken breast halves, boned, skinned, cut in 1 inch pieces
1/3 cup pine nuts
1/4 teaspoon cayenne pepper
1/4 teaspoon Beau Monde
1/4 teaspoon paprika
2 tablespoons butter
4 tablespoons olive oil
4 cloves garlic, pressed
1 1/4 cups chicken stock
1/2 cup white wine
1 tablespoon lemon juice
6 ounces dry linguine, cooked

---

serves 2

Preheat oven to 350 degrees. Roast pine nuts in a 6 inch omelette pan for 20 minutes, or until golden brown. Remove and lightly moisten with olive oil. Toss with cayenne pepper, Beau Monde and paprika, reserve.

In a 10 inch omelette pan, heat butter and oil. Add pressed garlic, then quickly sauté chicken. Remove chicken before it browns and set aside. Pour in chicken stock, white wine and lemon juice, reduce by one half. Return chicken to pan and reheat.

Pour chicken and sauce over hot pasta and toss. Sprinkle with spiced pine nuts.

pictured
risotto with corn & red pepper, 138
gazpacho salad, 43
veal & spinach ravioli, 134
with jeff's favorite tomato & garlic sauce, 136

R. MICHAEL KASPERZAK, JR.
Mountain View, California

OLIO

PAELLA

3 pound fryer chicken
5 rock lobster tails
1½ pounds large shrimp
1 dozen clams
1 can of minced clams
1 pound lean boneless pork
1 pound chorizo, or hot Italian sausage
4 tablespoons olive oil
3 large onions, chopped
4 green onions, chopped
3 cloves garlic, minced
5 cups chicken broth
2 grams of saffron
pinch of cayenne pepper
2 cups long grain rice
1 bay leaf
1 teaspoon shellfish seasoning
4 ounces pimentos
½ cup black olives, pitted, halved
1 can of artichoke hearts, diced
½ cup chopped fresh parsley
1 large tomato, peeled, seeded, diced

serves 10

Preheat oven to 350 degrees.

Cut chicken into pieces. Cut pork into 1 inch pieces.

Heat olive oil in a 16 inch paella pan on medium high heat. Add onions and garlic and cook until the onions are translucent. Add chicken pieces and brown. Remove chicken and onions. Add sausage to the paella pan and brown, remove and cut sausage into bite size pieces. Add the pork pieces and brown, remove. Put chicken, sausage, and pork in an ovenproof dish and place in oven until ready to use.

Add chicken stock, saffron and cayenne pepper to the paella pan, bring to a simmer. Add rice, chicken pieces and sausage and pork, cover, and place in oven for 30 minutes.

Boil water in a 4½ quart sauce pan, add lobster, bay leaf and shellfish seasoning. Cook for 12 minutes. Remove lobster, split lengthwise. Remove paella pan from oven and stir in pimento, minced clams, black olives and artichokes.

Add split lobster tails, clams and shrimp. Put paella in oven, cover, and cook for 15 minutes or until the clams have opened and shrimp is pink. Sprinkle top with fresh chopped parsley and chopped tomatoes.

Sara Jane Kasperzak

VEAL & SPINACH RAVIOLI

Ravioli's can be formed using a grid, or you can make your own ravioli shapes by hand. Many restaurants serve a single, four inch ravioli surrounded by sauce as a first course.

---

4 cups flour
4 eggs
1 tablespoon plus 1 teaspoon olive oil
pinch of salt
Veal and Spinach Filling
1 egg white

---

serves 6

Place 3 cups flour on board and make a well in center. Put 4 eggs, oil and salt into well. Using a fork, beat egg mixture slowly, working in flour from underneath. Work into a ball, then set aside. Dust surface with 1 cup of flour.

Knead dough by hand until it becomes elastic. Flatten ball, flour both sides and roll through pasta machine on widest setting. Place rolled sheet on a floured surface, fold into thirds then roll through machine again. Repeat this procedure several times, till dough is elastic and not too sticky. For final roll out, flour both sides of pasta sheet and roll through pasta machine. Lower the setting after each roll until desired thickness is achieved.

Using a ravioli form, lay a sheet of pasta across grid. Set impression plate over grid to make pockets. Place a tablespoon of Veal and Spinach Filling in each pocket. Brush pasta around filling with egg white. Place other sheet of pasta over filled pasta making sure air pockets are released. Seal and cut individual raviolis by rolling a rolling pin across grid.

Drop raviolis into boiling salted water and cook for 15 to 20 minutes or until tender. Remove and toss with Jeff's Favorite Tomato and Garlic Sauce.

VEAL AND SPINACH FILLING

---

10 ounces fresh leaf spinach, stems trimmed
1 tablespoon olive oil
1 pound ground veal
½ cup grated Parmesan cheese
¼ cup bread crumbs
3 tablespoons celery leaves, finely chopped
¼ teaspoon cinnamon
salt and pepper
1 egg

Bring 3 quarts salted water to boil. Add spinach and cook for 1 minute. Drain and squeeze water out of spinach. Pat dry with towel and chop fine.

Preheat a Calphalon 3 quart sauté pan on medium heat. Add olive oil, heat, then sauté veal until cooked through. Drain fat. In a large bowl thoroughly mix all ingredients except egg. In a separate bowl beat egg. Add to veal mixture and mix thoroughly.

Paul Angelo LoGiudice
Culinary Events Specialist
Commercial Aluminum Cookware Company

JEFF'S FAVORITE TOMATO & GARLIC SAUCE

This is a thick and chunky sauce that can be served over fusilli, penne, linguine, fettuccine, or your favorite pasta. It is also wonderful on homemade pizza, or with meatballs or ravioli.

---

5 tablespoons extra virgin olive oil
2½ cups coarsely chopped Spanish onion
5 large cloves garlic, finely chopped
2 35-ounce cans Italian peeled Pomidoro tomatoes, coarsely chopped with juice
6 ounces tomato paste
2 tablespoons finely chopped fresh basil leaves or 2 teaspoons dried basil
1 tablespoon dried oregano
1 small whole bay leaf
2 teaspoons sugar
1 teaspoon salt
½ teaspoon dried red pepper flakes (optional)
freshly ground black pepper

---

serves 4

Using a 4 quart Calphalon sauce pan, heat oil over medium heat, then sauté onion until transparent, 5 to 10 minutes. Add garlic and sauté 2 additional minutes. Stir in remaining ingredients. Bring sauce to a rolling boil, reduce heat to simmer. Simmer uncovered one hour, stirring occasionally. Remove bay leaf and correct seasonings.

Paula and Jeff Solinger
Solinger and Associates
Clarendon Hills, Illinois

RAVIOLI DI VERDURA AL' MASCARPONE

½ head white cabbage
2 pounds Swiss chard
2 pounds spinach
3 green onions, chopped
3 tablespoons butter
4 tablespoons grated Parmesan cheese
1 egg
3 tablespoons pine nuts
salt and pepper
pasta sheets for seven raviolis per serving
Basil Cheese Sauce
sliced roasted almonds

serves 6

Wash and coarsely chop cabbage, Swiss chard and spinach, combine and set aside. In a large pan, sauté green onion in butter until soft. Add cabbage, spinach and Swiss chard mixture and continue to sauté until all vegetables are soft. Cool and coarsely chop mixture, combine with Parmesan cheese and egg, blend well. Add pine nuts, blend. Set aside.

Divide each pasta sheet into 2 inch squares, setting aside 2 squares per ravioli. Put 1 tablespoon of filling in the center of one ravioli square, wet edges with water. Using other ravioli square, top and seal. Proceed with remainder of pasta squares and filling. Cook raviolis in boiling water for 4 to 5 minutes. Drain. Place raviolis on plate. Pour Basil Cheese Sauce over raviolis and garnish with roasted almonds.

BASIL CHEESE SAUCE

2 tablespoons butter
6 leaves fresh basil, chopped
2 cups heavy cream
8 ounces mascarpone cheese
2 tablespoons Parmesan cheese
salt and pepper

In a sauté pan, add butter and basil. Heat and pour in cream. Boil for 2 minutes.

Remove from heat and stir in the mascarpone and Parmesan cheese, mix well.

Laurence Mindel
Il Fornaio restaurant
San Francisco, California

RISOTTO WITH CORN & RED PEPPER

Ron loved traveling to Italy, especially Milan, where he could indulge in their delicious risottos, one of his favorite foods. Risotto, made with Italian Arborio rice, can be served as a first course or with a salad as an entree.

---

3 slices bacon, diced
2 shallots, chopped
2 cloves garlic, chopped
1½ cups Arborio rice
5 cups chicken broth
1 red bell pepper, cored, seeded, diced
1 ear of fresh corn, cut from the cob
⅓ cup chopped cilantro
4 ounces fresh goat cheese
½ cup grated Monterey Jack cheese

---

serves 4

Sauté bacon until crisp in a pan. Remove bacon and drain excess grease on paper towel. Sauté shallots and garlic in bacon fat. When shallots and garlic are light brown, add Arborio rice and stir until coated with bacon drippings and rice starts to brown.

Meanwhile in a 2 quart sauce pan bring chicken broth to a boil, reduce heat and simmer.

Pour ½ cup of heated broth into the rice and continue stirring. When the rice is almost dry, add another ½ cup of broth and continue stirring rice. Continue this process until broth is gone, about 20 minutes. Five minutes before the last ½ cup of broth is added, stir in the bacon, red pepper, corn, cilantro and goat cheese. Toss before serving with Monterey Jack cheese.

DOUG MCNATTON
Barbara Boyle and Associates
Los Angeles, California

RISOTTO WITH PORCINI & FRESH BASIL

Porcini mushrooms are abundant in Italy in their fresh state. Fortunately, their unique flavor is retained in the dried version, available at specialty stores and many supermarkets. The flavor is then released by soaking them in hot water.

2/3 ounce dried porcini mushrooms
3 1/2 cups chicken stock
2 tablespoons olive oil
3/4 cup finely chopped onions
3 cloves garlic, finely chopped
1 cup Arborio Rice
3 tablespoons finely chopped fresh basil
1/4 cup grated Parmesan cheese
1/4 cup grated Romano cheese
salt and pepper

---

serves 4-6

Soak dried porcini mushrooms in 1 cup of hot water for 30 minutes. Remove mushrooms from water and chop finely. Strain and reserve water.

In a Calphalon 1 1/2 quart sauce pan, bring chicken stock to a boil, reduce heat and simmer.

Preheat a Calphalon 2 quart sauteuse pan on medium heat. Add olive oil and heat 1 minute, then sauté onions and garlic for 2 to 3 minutes. Add rice and sauté for 3 to 4 minutes. Stir 1/2 cup of hot chicken stock into rice mixture. Continue stirring until stock is absorbed. Add remaining stock, 1/3 cup at a time, stirring until all stock is absorbed.

Add porcini mushrooms, basil and 1/4 cup of the reserved water. Stir until water is absorbed. Add remaining reserved water, 1/4 cup at a time, stirring until absorbed. Stir Parmesan and Romano cheese into mixture. Season with salt and pepper.

Paul Angelo LoGiudice
Culinary Events Specialist
Commercial Aluminum Cookware Company

VEGETABLE DISHES

ASPARAGUS IN PROSCIUTTO

2 pounds asparagus
13 ounces chicken broth
olive oil
4 slices prosciutto
6 tablespoons butter
1/3 cup Bel Paese cheese, grated
1/4 cup Madeira wine

serves 4

Preheat oven to 400 degrees.

Snap off tough ends of fresh asparagus. Tie into 4 bundles of 4 to 6 spears and stand upright in the bottom pan of a double boiler. Pour chicken broth to cover lower half of stalks. Cover with inverted double boiler insert, steam until tender. Do not overcook.

Grease baking dish lightly with olive oil. Wrap 1 slice of prosciutto around each bunch of cooked, tied asparagus and arrange, fold side down, in bottom of dish. Place a dab of butter on each bundle's tips. Sprinkle lightly with Bel Paese cheese. Pour wine into bottom of pan. Bake until the cheese melts and sizzles.

Judy Glassberg
TAG
Chicago, Illinois

CARCIOFI ALLÁ SICILIANA

SICILIAN ARTICHOKES

---

4 artichokes
lemon juice
1½ cups bread crumbs
⅓ cup olive oil
¾ cup grated Parmesan cheese
⅓ cup grated Romano cheese
1½ tablespoons basil
1 tablespoon oregano
¼ cup finely chopped parsley
3 cloves garlic, finely chopped
salt and pepper

---

serves 4

Remove outer leaves at the bottom of the artichokes, then slice ¾ inch off the top of each artichoke removing the majority of the hard tips. Using kitchen shears cut pointed ends off the remaining leaves. To prevent the cut leaf ends from discoloring, dip the top of the artichoke into lemon juice. Cut off stem at the base to form a flat bottom. Spread leaves by turning artichoke upside down and pushing base down with the palm of your hand.

Preheat a Calphalon 10 inch omelette pan on medium heat. Add bread crumbs and stir until golden, then stir in olive oil. In a large bowl mix bread crumbs, cheese and remaining ingredients. Season with salt and pepper. Stuff each artichoke by spooning a heaping teaspoon of stuffing into each opened leaf, working from the outside leaves toward the center. Make sure stuffing is pushed to the base of each leaf.

Place stuffed artichokes in a Calphalon 5 quart saucier pan with 1 cup salted water. Sprinkle top of artichokes with olive oil. Bring water to a simmer, cover, and cook for 1 hour or until a leaf can be easily removed. Check water and replenish if needed.

PAUL ANGELO LOGIUDICE
Culinary Events Specialist
Commercial Aluminum Cookware Company

CHEESY GARDEN CASSEROLE

When the garden is peaking with vegetables this casserole is good to remember. You can vary the recipe to use the vegetables that are most abundant, or your family's favorites. The marinara sauce can be your own version, or try Jeff's Favorite Tomato and Garlic Sauce.

---

2 cups cooked brown rice
2 cups broccoli, cut into 1/2 inch slices
2 carrots, cut in strips
1 zucchini, bias sliced
1 cup cut green beans
10 ounces marinara sauce
1 cup shredded longhorn or mild cheddar
1 cup shredded Monterey Jack cheese

---

serves 6

Preheat oven to 375 degrees.

Place cooked rice in bottom of an oval au gratin pan. Cook broccoli, carrots, zucchini and green beans in boiling salt water until just tender, 5 to 7 minutes. Drain. Reserve four zucchini slices for garnish. Spoon remaining vegetables over rice. Top with marinara sauce. Cover and bake for 30 minutes. Combine cheeses and sprinkle over casserole. Return to oven to melt cheese about 5 minutes. Garnish with reserved zucchini slices.

MARILYN MASLOW
Dallas, Pennsylvania

CORN CAKES

Corn cakes can be served as a side dish or as an appetizer with sour cream, fresh salsa, and minced onion. Try substituting corn cakes for corn bread and serve with a hot, spicy chili.

---

2 eggs
3 tablespoons sweet unsalted butter
1 cup cornmeal
7 ounces corn, drained
3/4 cup milk

---

yields 18-36

Combine ingredients in blender, blending until batter reaches the desired consistency. Spoon the batter onto a preheated greased griddle. Cook until edges are dry and top is bubbling, turn and cook other side until golden. Corn cakes can be made the size of silver dollars or larger. Serve immediately.

ROSELEE C. NICHOLS
Old Greenwich, Connecticut

POTATOES GRUYÈRE

---

8 to 10 medium russet potatoes, peeled
¾ pound Gruyère cheese, grated
2 tablespoons minced fresh dill
salt and pepper
¼ cup unsalted butter
10 ounces chicken broth

---

serves 8

Preheat oven to 375 degrees. Butter bottom and sides of 13 inch Calphalon au gratin pan.

Slice peeled potatoes thinly using a 3mm blade on food processor. Immediately place sliced potatoes in ice water to avoid discoloration. Drain potatoes and pat dry with paper towel. Line bottom of buttered pan with half of potatoes, overlapping on top of each other. Sprinkle with half of cheese and dill. Season lightly with salt and pepper. Repeat with another layer of potatoes and remaining cheese and dill. Season again with salt and pepper. Slice butter into thin pats and place on top. Pour chicken broth over everything.

Place in oven and bake for 45 minutes. Cool 5 to 10 minutes. Serve hot.

Jim Salveson
Los Angeles, California

POTATOES ROMANOFF

Potatoes Romanoff is a dish that falls into the category of "comfort foods". It is a new version of an old favorite - twice baked potatoes.

---

6 cups cooked, cubed new potatoes, skins on
2 cups cottage cheese
1 cup sour cream
1 clove garlic, minced
5 tablespoons chopped chives
1½ cups shredded cheddar cheese

---

serves 8

Preheat oven to 350 degrees. Grease a 3 quart casserole.

Combine all ingredients, reserving ½ cup cheddar cheese. Pour into greased casserole.

Cover and bake for 30 minutes. Uncover, sprinkle with remaining cheese, and bake 5 minutes.

CAREY HEWITT
The Cupboard
Fort Collins, Colorado

SWEET POTATO PANCAKES

Served as part of a California Thanksgiving meal, this is a new and interesting way to prepare traditional holiday sweet potatoes.

---

2 pounds sweet potatoes, red garnet or red yams (about 6 to 8)
1/4 cup golden raisins
1/2 cup brown sugar
1/4 cup unbleached flour
1/2 teaspoon cinnamon
1/4 teaspoon nutmeg
1/2 cup chopped walnuts
1 tablespoon butter

---

serves 8

Peel potatoes and cover with water in a 4 1/2 quart Calphalon sauce pan. Bring to a boil. After boiling for 10 minutes, immediately run potatoes under cold water. Grate potatoes.

In a large mixing bowl, combine remaining ingredients, except for butter. Fold in grated potatoes, mix thoroughly.

Cut a large piece of parchment paper. Make pancakes with 2 tablespoons of potato mixture. Flatten out on parchment paper.

Preheat a Calphalon griddle on medium heat. When hot, add 1 tablespoon of butter. Butter should be briskly bubbling, but not burning. Tear parchment paper around each potato patty and invert onto griddle. Peel off paper. Cook on each side 3 to 4 minutes or until golden and crisp on surface.

Paul Angelo LoGiudice
Culinary Events Specialist
Commercial Aluminum Cookware Company

TOMATO PUDDING

This dish was adapted from a recipe from the kitchen of President Dwight D. Eisenhower. The unique and delicious taste is always a surprise for those tasting it for the first time.

---

10 ounces tomato puree
1/4 cup boiling water
6 tablespoons dark brown sugar
2 cups white bread, cubed
1/4 cup melted butter or margarine

---

serves 4

Preheat oven to 375 degrees.

Mix puree, sugar and water in a Calphalon 1 1/2 quart sauce pan. Boil 5 minutes. Place bread cubes in a casserole dish. Melt butter and pour over bread cubes. Pour puree mixture over bread cubes. Bake uncovered for 30 minutes.

Holly Wynn Borden
Koehler Borden, Inc.
North Canton, Ohio

ZUCCHINI SOUFFLÉ

Vegetable soufflés were a favorite of Ron's. You can vary the vegetables and cheeses for a change of flavor. Soufflés are a wonderful way to get children to eat vegetables. This soufflé can be frozen unbaked.

---

3 cups grated zucchini
1 large onion, chopped
1 clove garlic
4 eggs
½ cup vegetable or olive oil
2 teaspoons Italian herbs
1 teaspoon salt
pepper
1 cup Bisquick
1 cup grated Parmesan cheese

---

serves 8

Preheat oven to 350 degrees.

In food processor, grate the zucchini and put in large bowl. Using knife blade, chop garlic and onion medium fine and add to zucchini. Without washing processor, beat eggs and oil and add to zucchini mixture together with herbs, salt, pepper, ½ cup Parmesan cheese and Bisquick. Pour into au gratin pan.

Top with the remaining ½ cup of Parmesan cheese. Bake 45 to 50 minutes until set and cheese is browned.

FRANCES ENSLEIN
Frances Enslein Cooking School
Greenwich, Connecticut

BRUNCH & BREADS

ALMOND PECAN COFFEE CAKE

Your family will enjoy the various options Danish pastry offers. Make coffee cakes or individual pastry twists filled with your favorite jams or preserves.

1/2 recipe Danish Pastry
1/2 recipe Almond Pecan Cream Filling, or other filling
1 egg white
1/4 cup finely chopped pecans
2 cups sifted powdered sugar
1 teaspoon vanilla
1/3 cup water or milk

---

makes 1 coffee cake

Roll chilled dough into a 10x10 inch square. Spread pecan filling over two thirds of the rolled dough surface, leaving one third free along one side. Fold into thirds, folding plain side first. Press edges to seal.

Cut dough lengthwise into 3 strips. Take 1 strip, twist slightly, then starting in the center of a greased 8 inch round cake pan coil to start a pinwheel. Take second strip, continue coiling where the first strip left off. Repeat with the third strip. Coil loosely so the dough has room to expand. With a fork, mix egg white with 2 tablespoons water, brush over rolls. Let rise 1 hour, or overnight, in the refrigerator. Before baking sprinkle with half of chopped pecans. Preheat oven to 375 degrees and bake for 25 minutes or until lightly browned.

Mix powdered sugar, vanilla and milk until smooth, adding milk a tablespoon at a time. Brush over surface of coffee cake. Sprinkle with remaining pecans. Cool in pan or on rack. Cut into wedges to serve.

ALMOND PECAN CREAM FILLING

1/4 cup butter
1 1/4 cup sifted powdered sugar
1 tablespoon flour
1 egg yolk
1 to 2 drops almond extract
1/4 cup finely chopped pecans

Cream together butter, powdered sugar and flour. Beat in egg yolk and almond extract. Stir in pecans.

DANISH PASTRY

1 package active dry yeast
1/4 cup warm water
1 cup butter
3 tablespoons sugar
1/2 teaspoon salt
1 egg
1/2 cup milk
3 cups sifted flour

yields dough for 2 coffee cakes

Dissolve yeast in warm water and refrigerate 10 minutes. Meanwhile, cream 1/4 cup butter with sugar and salt. Add egg and beat well. Stir in milk and yeast mixture. Add flour a little at a time and continue mixing until flour is moistened and forms a soft dough, just firm enough to handle. Turn dough onto a floured pastry cloth and knead until it is smooth and elastic, working more flour into dough as needed.

Pat dough into a 1/2 inch thick square. Fold all four sides to center. Turn dough over and pat down to another square and repeat. Wrap loosely in wax paper and place in refrigerator for 10 minutes. While dough chills, cut remaining butter into 30 pats.

Return dough to pastry cloth. Roll out into a rectangle about 3/4 inch thick keeping corners as square as possible. Place half of the thin butter pats side by side on the center third of the dough, fold one side of the dough over. Press edges together. Place remaining butter squares on top of the folded portion. Fold the other third of the dough over the top, press edges together. Roll out dough into a rectangle. The rolling should be smooth and even in order to form unbroken alternate layers of butter and dough. Fold in thirds again and roll out into a rectangle. Fold in thirds once more. Wrap tightly, and chill overnight.

Rebecca Hetrick
Commercial Aluminum Cookware Company
Toledo, Ohio

CHEESE BREAD

This Cheese Bread is featured in THE ART OF COOKING, VOLUME 2. Jacques Pepin explains that a proof box can be created by inserting a trimmed cardboard box into a large plastic bag. When the bag is closed you will have a humid hot house similar to a professional proof box.

---

1 cup milk
1 package active dry yeast or 1 cake fresh yeast
1 teaspoon sugar
3 cups bread flour
1 teaspoon salt
6 tablespoons butter
2 eggs
2 cups grated sharp cheddar cheese
1 cup dried pears, cut into 1/4 inch pieces
egg wash made with 1 egg with half the white removed, beaten
1 tablespoon oatmeal (not instant)

---

makes 1 large loaf

Heat milk to about 95 degrees and add the yeast and sugar. Combine gently and proof for 10 minutes in the bowl of a mixer.

Add flour, salt, butter, eggs and using the dough hook, beat on medium speed for about 5 minutes. Add the grated cheese and dried pears, and mix about 30 seconds to 1 minute, just long enough to incorporate. Cover the bowl with plastic wrap and let the dough rise at room temperature for 1 1/2 hours.

At that point, the dough will be well risen. Fold the dough in on itself from the sides toward the center and press to deflate.

Butter a 3 quart charlotte mold and arrange the dough in it. Place in a proof box or cover with a towel and let rise in a warm area for 1 hour.

Preheat oven to 400 degrees. Brush dough with egg wash. Sprinkle with the oatmeal and slash two lines with a razor blade across the surface of the loaf. Bake on the center rack for 15 minutes, then reduce heat to 350 degrees and continue baking for another 20 minutes.

Remove bread from the oven and keep in a warm place for 15 to 20 minutes so the dough doesn't soften and collapse on itself. Allow the bread to rest 1 hour before slicing. The center should look buttery and have a yeasty, cheesy smell.

JACQUES PEPIN
Board Member of the American Institute of Wine and Food
Member of the International Association of Culinary Professionals
Madison, Connecticut

ENGLISH MUFFINS

The dough can be cut into different shapes, a fun task for children to do. Beating dough well during the mixing stage cuts down on kneading time. Don't be afraid to overbeat.

---

1 cup milk
3 tablespoons sugar
1 teaspoon salt
1/4 cup margarine or butter
1 cup warm water
1 package yeast
5 1/2 cups flour
cornmeal

---

makes 20 muffins

In a sauce pan, scald milk and combine with sugar, salt and margarine. Cook until lukewarm. In a large bowl, add warm water and sprinkle with yeast. Stir until dissolved. Add milk mixture and stir. Add half of flour and beat with an electric mixer. Continue adding flour until mixture is a soft dough.

Place small amount of flour, 1/2 cup to 3/4 cup, on a board or canvas type cloth and turn dough on top. Knead until smooth and elastic, 8 to 10 minutes. Place dough in a greased bowl and lightly oil the top of it. Cover with a damp cloth. Let rise in a warm place until double, about 1 hour.

Punch down dough and divide in half. Sprinkle the canvas cloth heavily with cornmeal. Roll dough to about 1/2 inch thickness and cut with a 3 inch round cutter, or cut in squares with a sharp knife. Cover with a damp cloth and let rise 30 minutes.

Lightly grease griddle and heat in oven until griddle is medium hot. Carefully place each muffin on griddle cornmeal side down. Bake until bottom is well browned, about 12 minutes. Turn and bake for 12 minutes on the second side. Muffins may be frozen. When ready to serve, split and toast.

Ginny Gordon
Ginny Gordon Gifts and Gadgets
Beauford, North Carolina

CORNMEAL CRÊPES
WITH PAPAYA CREAM FILLING AND GRAPEFRUIT GLAZE

Crêpes can be rolled or folded, filled with your favorite seasonal fruit. Because this batter doesn't store well it should be used immediately.

---

2 eggs
1/3 cup light brown sugar
4 tablespoons sweet unsalted butter, melted
1 cup yellow cornmeal
3/4 cup milk
peanut oil
Papaya Cream Filling
Grapefruit Glaze

---

serves 6

Blend eggs and sugar to a smooth ribbon state. Mix in butter. Add cornmeal and blend until smooth. Stir in milk, let batter stand for 10 minutes.

Preheat a Calphalon crêpe pan on medium heat. When pan is heated, lightly oil the cooking surface. Pour in 1/3 cup of batter, tilting pan to cover bottom. Pour off excess. Return to heat. After a minute, or when crêpe has a light golden color on bottom, slide spatula under crêpe and turn. Cook the other side for 10 to 15 seconds. Place cooked crêpe between sheets of wax paper. Repeat process for remainder of batter. Cover with a towel to keep crêpes moist and flexible.

To assemble crêpes, place about 3 to 4 tablespoons of chilled Papaya Cream Filling on end of crêpe, and roll up. Place on serving plate, drizzle cooled Grapefruit Glaze over crêpe, garnish with a slice of papaya and a mint leaf. Sprinkle top with grapefruit zest.

PAPAYA CREAM FILLING

6 ounces fresh papaya, peeled, seeded
1 cup half and half
4 egg yolks
⅔ cup sugar
4 tablespoons flour

Puree papaya in food processor, set aside. In a sauce pan, heat half and half to almost boiling. In a mixing bowl, beat egg yolks and sugar to a smooth ribbon state. Gradually mix in flour, add ½ cup of the heated half and half a little at a time.

Add mixture to the remaining half and half. Bring to a soft boil and allow pastry cream to thicken, about 4 to 5 minutes. Remove from heat and blend in papaya. Chill until ready to assemble crêpes.

GRAPEFRUIT GLAZE

¼ cup sugar
1 cup grapefruit juice
¼ cup lime juice
¼ cup Triple Sec

On medium high heat, melt sugar in a Calphalon 1½ quart Windsor sauce pan, stirring occasionally. Cook until light golden in color (carmelized), about 8 to 10 minutes.

Add remaining ingredients, bring to a boil and reduce by one half, or until thick and syrupy. Cool before serving.

Paul Angelo LoGiudice
Culinary Events Specialist
Commercial Aluminum Cookware Company

FRITTATA

ITALIAN VEGETABLE OMELETTE

Frittatas are great to make ahead and freeze. It is fun to experiment with different ingredients and herbs to invent your own version. Karen suggested serving this for a brunch with apple muffins. For a light dinner, serve it with Italian bread spread with olive oil, garlic powder, Italian seasoning and mozzarella cheese heated under the broiler.

---

3 tablespoons olive oil
1 large potato, diced into 1/4 inch pieces
1/2 cup chopped onion
1/2 cup sliced mushrooms
1/2 small zucchini, julienned
1/2 to 1 teaspoon salt
freshly ground pepper
6 eggs or 1 1/2 cups egg substitute
1/2 teaspoon Italian seasoning
1/4 cup freshly grated Romano cheese

---

serves 4

Place olive oil in a Calphalon 10 inch omelette pan, or pan with a metal handle, heat on medium. Swirl olive oil to coat bottom and sides. Sauté potatoes for 5 minutes. Add mushrooms and onions and sauté 5 minutes. Add zucchini and sauté 2 minutes.

Preheat the broiler. Beat eggs with the Italian seasoning and 2 tablespoons of Romano cheese. Lightly salt and pepper the vegetables, then pour the egg mixture over the vegetables. Cook over medium heat about 10 minutes, shaking the pan frequently.

Sprinkle remaining Romano cheese over the top, lightly salt and pepper to taste, and place under the broiler until the cheese is lightly brown. Eggs should be completely set. Cut in wedges, serve and garnish with cherry tomatoes and parsley.

Karen C. Brown
Kitchen Wavelengths
Toledo, Ohio

FRITTATA AROMATICA

OMELETTE WITH HERBS

When Judy used a Calphalon omelette pan for the first time, she was immediately convinced that Calphalon should be available to cooking enthusiasts outside of the restaurant and foodservice industry. Through her efforts she persuaded Ron to market to home cooks and she became the first retail account.

---

4 tablespoons unsalted butter
1/2 pound spinach, cleaned, chopped
1/4 bunch parsley, stems discarded, leaves chopped
1/4 bunch basil, stems discarded, leaves chopped
7 eggs
1 teaspoon salt
1/4 teaspoon pepper

---

serves 4-6

Heat butter in a 10 inch Calphalon omelette pan, and cook spinach, parsley and basil over medium heat for 3 minutes.

Mix the eggs lightly in a bowl with salt and pepper, pour over the herbs and cook over medium heat until mixture begins to set, about 5 or 6 minutes. Place a plate upside down over the frittata, and holding the plate and pan together, turn pan quickly upside down over the plate. Slip the frittata, cooked side up, from the plate into the frying pan and cook about 2 minutes longer to set the underside. Serve immediately.

JUDITH ETS-HOKIN
Culinary Company
Author of THE HOME CHEF and THE SAN FRANCISCO DINNER PARTY COOKBOOK
Member of International Association of Culinary Professionals
San Francisco, California

HILDA'S SPINNEY BREAD

This cornmeal based bread has a wonderful texture and is especially good toasted.

1/4 cup yellow cornmeal
water
6 cups flour
1 teaspoon salt
1/4 cup sugar
1 package dry yeast

makes 2 loaves

Put cornmeal in a bowl and mix with 1 cup boiling water, cool. Combine flour, salt and sugar and stir into cornmeal. In another bowl combine 1/4 cup warm water and yeast, proof for 10 minutes, then mix into cornmeal mixture. Add two cups cold water and mix to form a soft dough. Cover and let rise 1 hour in a warm place.

Punch down dough and divide it into 2 buttered loaf pans. Cover and let rise again in a warm place for about 1 hour. Preheat oven to 425 degrees and bake 30 minutes. Reduce oven temperature to 350 degrees and continue baking for 20 minutes.

Robin Muzzy
Perrysburg, Ohio

IRISH BROWN BREAD

Ron's son, Joel, and his wife, Laura, lived in Ireland for the first three years of their marriage. During her stay Laura became an expert at Irish breads.

---

2 cups whole wheat flour
1 cup unbleached flour
1 teaspoon baking soda
1 teaspoon salt
2 tablespoons light brown sugar
2 tablespoons melted butter or margarine
1 cup lowfat buttermilk plus extra as needed

---

makes 1 loaf

Preheat oven to 325 degrees.

Mix ingredients very well, leaving the buttermilk until last. Start with a cup of buttermilk, adding a little more until the consistency is sticky. Knead lightly on a floured board, then place in a greased and floured 5x9 loaf pan. Bake for one hour. Wrap immediately in a clean tea towel to prevent the crust from hardening too much.

LAURA KASPERZAK
Atlanta, Georgia

ORANGE SLICES IN CHAMPAGNE-GINGER SAUCE

Ron loved fruit at the end of a meal and enjoyed dining in Europe where interesting fresh fruit was always available. Chef Hovis of Macy's, New York shared his favorite fruit recipe with us.

---

8 large naval oranges
1 cup ginger marmalade
1 cup stem ginger in syrup
½ cup superfine sugar
2 cups dry champagne
½ cup slivered almonds, toasted

---

serves 6-8

Using a sharp knife, peel oranges, removing all of the white pith. Slice oranges into ¼ inch rounds. Place in a glass bowl.

In the container of a blender or food processor, with the steel blade in place, combine ginger marmalade, stem ginger, sugar and champagne. (If you are using a large bottle, I suggest you consider drinking the rest.) Process until completely smooth.

Pour the mixture over oranges, cover with plastic wrap, and refrigerate overnight. Turn the oranges occasionally.

Before serving, toast the almonds lightly. This may be done either in a 350 degree oven or on top of the stove with a scant teaspoon of oil, shaking the pan often. Sprinkle oranges with almonds.

GENE HOVIS
Macy's
Author of UPTOWN DOWN HOME cookbook
New York, New York

PLETTA

GRANDMOTHER'S SWEDISH PANCAKES

Serve pletta the traditional Swedish way with butter and sugar for brunch. They are also good with sliced strawberries or raspberries and lightly dusted with powdered sugar, or served with a dollop of whip cream for dessert. Using Bisquick will make the pletta puffy, while using all flour will make them thin like crêpes.

---

2 eggs
2 cups milk
½ teaspoon salt
2 teaspoons sugar
1 cup flour
½ cup Bisquick, or another ½ cup flour
butter

---

makes 4 large or 32 silver dollar size pancakes

Heat griddle.

In a medium size bowl, beat eggs. Continue to beat while adding milk, salt and sugar. Add dry ingredients a little at a time, while continuing to beat. The batter should be thin. Use a little butter to grease a hot griddle. Pletta can be made the size of silver dollars or larger for roll up pancakes.

JERRY ROWLETTE
Rowlette and Associates
Long Lake, Minnesota

pictured
crunchy gazpacho soup, 34
cornmeal crêpes with papaya cream filling & grapefruit glaze, 156
borscht, 27

RICE CALAS

The word "cala" comes from an African word for rice and refers to a deep fried pastry made with rice, yeast, sugar, and spices. Serve calas for breakfast or as a dessert.

---

6 tablespoons flour
3 heaping tablespoons sugar
2 teaspoons baking powder
¼ teaspoon salt
pinch of nutmeg
¼ teaspoon vanilla
2 cups cooked rice
2 eggs
powdered sugar

---

serves 6

Heat 4 inches of oil in deep pan, or flat bottom wok to 360 degrees.

Mix together flour, sugar, baking powder, salt and nutmeg in a bowl. In another bowl beat the vanilla, cooked rice and eggs.

Combine dry ingredients with rice mixture. When thoroughly mixed, drop by spoonfuls into hot oil and fry until brown. Drain on paper towels. Sprinkle with powdered sugar and serve hot.

POPPY TOOKER
Walter Davis, Inc.
New Orleans, Louisiana

MIMI'S CINNAMON ROLLS & COFFEE CAKE

This potato based recipe has been handed down from generation to generation. This is a family favorite for special celebrations and holidays.

Mimi's Basic Dough
3 tablespoons cinnamon
2 cups sugar
1 cup butter

---

makes 2 coffee cakes

Mix cinnamon with sugar. Melt butter.

For cinnamon rolls: cut 3 ounce pieces of dough, dip in melted butter, pull into long strips and roll in cinnamon and sugar, tie into knot and place on greased baking sheet.

For coffee cake: divide dough in half. Separate each half into 3 sections. Dip each section in melted butter and pull into long strips. Roll in cinnamon and sugar and braid 3 sections together to make each coffee cake. Place on greased baking sheet.

Let the rolls or coffee cakes rise, covered with a cotton towel, until almost double in bulk, about 1½ hours. Preheat oven to 400 degrees and bake for 15 minutes or until done. While still warm, brush with lemon glaze.

MIMI'S BASIC DOUGH

½ cup mashed potatoes
2 cups milk, scalded
½ cup sugar
½ cup vegetable oil
1 package active dry yeast
¼ cup warm water, 105 -115 degrees
8 cups flour
1 teaspoon baking powder
½ teaspoon baking soda
1 teaspoon salt

yields dough for 2 coffee cakes

For mashed potatoes use 2½ inch, new red skinned potatoes that have been cooked, cooled and mashed with 2 tablespoons milk.

Scald milk, add sugar, oil and mashed potatoes. Mix together and let cool. In a large bowl, dissolve yeast in warm water for 3 to 5 minutes. Sift flour, baking powder, soda and salt, set aside.

Stir the potato mixture into yeast, then add 6 cups of flour, 2 cups at a time, mix thoroughly. Work in remaining 2 cups of flour by tossing dough on a floured board and kneading well, until smooth and elastic. Place dough in a greased bowl, turn the dough over once and cover with waxed paper or foil. Weight dough down with a plate. Dough may be kept chilled up to 5 days before using.

As needed, remove from refrigerator and rest dough covered 30 minutes. Punch dough down to allow gases to escape.

LEMON GLAZE

1¼ cups powdered sugar
¼ cup lemon juice
1 teaspoon vanilla

yields 1¼ cups

Mix all ingredients until smooth. Spread directly on warm rolls or coffee cakes.

SUSAN REAMS
Perrysburg, Ohio

STRAWBERRY BREAD

Flavored breads are wonderful served with salads. They are also an easy but attractive item to bake when asked to contribute to a bake sale.

---

3 cups flour
1 teaspoon salt
1 teaspoon baking soda
1 tablespoon cinnamon
2 cups sugar
3 eggs, slightly beaten
1½ cups vegetable oil
3 cups fresh strawberries, cleaned, chopped
1¼ cups chopped nut meats

Preheat oven to 350 degrees. Grease 2 loaf pans 5x9 inches.

Combine and mix all dry ingredients in a large bowl. Make a well in the center of the dry ingredients, add eggs and oil to center of well, and stir only to moisten. Gently fold in strawberries and nuts. Divide batter evenly between prepared pans. Bake for 60 minutes. Cool in pans 5 minutes, then turn out on side of rack to finish cooling.

Courtesy of Dick Sutton
Casey's restaurant
Williamsburg, Virginia

TORTILLA DE PATATA

POTATO AND ONION OMELETTE

Flat omelettes, sometimes called pancake omelettes, differ from traditional omelettes in two ways. First, they are always flat, not folded, and second, the filling is always mixed in with the eggs. In Spain, they are called tortillas and in Italy frittatas.

1/4 cup olive oil
3 large potatoes (1 1/2 pounds), peeled, sliced
1 medium onion, finely chopped
2 teaspoons salt
4 tablespoons unsalted butter
6 eggs

---

serves 4-6

Heat oil in 3 quart sauté pan, add potatoes, sprinkle with 1 teaspoon salt and turn potatoes in the pan to coat well with oil. Continue cooking, until potatoes brown lightly, then add onions, reduce the heat and cook about 10 minutes, stirring occasionally. The potatoes should be tender. Transfer to paper towels to drain.

Melt butter in a 10 inch omelette pan. Mix eggs lightly in a bowl with remaining salt. Stir in potatoes and onions. Pour omelette mixture into the pan, spread it out with a spatula and cook over moderate heat, 2 minutes. Cover pan with a flat plate and, grasping plate and pan firmly together, invert them and turn the omelette out onto the plate. Then carefully slide omelette back into pan, cooked side up, and cook 3 to 4 minutes longer to set the underside. Serve at once.

JUDITH ETS-HOKIN
Culinary Company
Author of THE HOME CHEF and THE SAN FRANCISCO DINNER PARTY COOKBOOK
Member of the International Association of Culinary Professionals
San Francisco, California

DESSERTS & PASTRIES

BLUE RIBBON BLUEBERRY CRUMB CAKE
WITH TANGY YOGURT CREAM

This cake can be baked a day ahead, then covered and set aside at room temperature. Refrigerate the yogurt cream, if making ahead.

2½ cups blueberries, about 1 pint
½ teaspoon grated lemon zest
2¼ cups flour
1 cup sugar
¾ cup unsalted butter, cut into small pieces
1 teaspoon baking soda
1 egg
½ cup plain low fat yogurt
1 teaspoon fresh lemon juice
Tangy Yogurt Cream

---

serves 8

Preheat oven to 400 degrees. Butter a round 10x1½ inch baking dish or a 10 inch springform pan.

In a medium bowl, mix blueberries with lemon zest. In a large bowl, combine 2 cups of the flour with the sugar. Using your fingertips or a pastry blender, cut butter into the dry ingredients until mixture resembles coarse meal. Set 1½ cups of mixture aside for the crumb topping.

In a small bowl, combine remaining ¼ cup flour with the baking soda and mix well. Add to mealy mixture in the large bowl, and with pastry blender, cut the flour into mixture until incorporated.

In a small bowl, lightly beat the egg. Stir in the yogurt and lemon juice. Add to dry ingredients in large bowl and stir briefly with a wooden spoon until blended. Fold in 1 cup of blueberries.

Spread batter in the prepared dish and scatter the remaining 1½ cups blueberries on top. Sprinkle the reserved crumb mixture over the blueberries. Set the dish on a cookie sheet and bake in the middle of the oven for about 1 hour, or until crumbs are golden and a tester inserted in the center of the cake comes out clean. Serve warm or at room temperature with Tangy Yogurt Cream.

TANGY YOGURT CREAM

1 cup heavy cream, chilled
2 tablespoons sugar
1 teaspoon lemon juice
⅓ cup plain low fat yogurt

In a medium bowl, combine all the ingredients and beat until stiff. Transfer the cream to a serving bowl and refrigerate, covered, for at least 30 minutes before serving.

Diana Sturgis
Test Kitchen Director, FOOD & WINE magazine
New York, New York

BANANA CAKE

Delightful plain, or topped with your favorite cream cheese frosting.

½ cup butter
1¼ cups sugar
2 eggs
1 teaspoon baking soda
4 heaping tablespoons sour cream
1 cup banana pulp mashed (3 medium, ripe bananas)
1½ cups flour
¼ teaspoon salt
1 teaspoon vanilla

Preheat oven to 350 degrees. Butter a 9x13 inch bake pan.

In a large bowl, cream butter with sugar until light and fluffy. Lightly beat eggs and add to the butter and sugar.

Mix baking soda with sour cream, then add to the batter. Mix batter thoroughly with wooden spoon. Add bananas, flour, salt and vanilla. Mix well. Pour into prepared pan and bake about 45 minutes or until done.

Marilyn Maslow
Dallas, Pennsylvania

CHOCOLATE MOUSSE TORTE

The perfect finale to a dinner party, this wonderful rich dessert tastes incredible. It is easy to make and freezes well.

---

7 ounces semisweet chocolate
2 tablespoons unsalted butter
½ cup plus 2 tablespoons sugar
7 egg yolks
7 egg whites
2 cups whipping cream
1 to 2 tablespoons powdered sugar
1 to 2 tablespoons Grand Marnier

---

serves 8-10

Preheat oven to 325 degrees.

Melt chocolate and butter together, cool. Beat ½ cup sugar and egg yolks in medium bowl for 3 minutes at high speed, until creamy. Add cooled chocolate.

In another bowl, beat egg whites until soft peaks form. Add 2 tablespoons sugar and beat until stiff peaks form. Fold egg whites into chocolate batter.

Pour ¾ cup of batter into an 8 or 9 inch ungreased springform pan. Bake for 35 minutes. Remove from oven and let torte cool and fall. Run knife around edge to loosen. Pour remaining mousse over center of baked torte and chill until cold.

When ready to serve, release side of pan and remove. Whip cream, adding the powdered sugar and Grand Marnier to taste. Spread over cold torte or use pastry bag to decorate top with rosettes. Garnish with chocolate leaves, cookie crumbs or sliced fresh strawberries. Serve cold.

Barbara Dunn
Village Kitchen Shoppe & Gourmet Market
Glendora, California

CHOCOLATE MOUSSE CAKE

The Génoise base can be made a day ahead of assembling and refrigerated, or prepared weeks ahead and frozen.

GÉNOISE

3 eggs
½ cup sugar
½ cup flour
¼ cup unsweetened cocoa powder (Drosti)
1 teaspoon baking soda
2 tablespoons melted butter, lukewarm
1 teaspoon vanilla
Raspberry Syrup
Chocolate Cream
bittersweet chocolate
unsweetened cocoa powder
1 pint whipping cream
3 tablespoons powdered sugar
½ teaspoon vanilla

serves 8

Preheat oven to 350 degrees. Grease a 9 inch springform cake pan. Line the bottom with parchment or waxed paper, grease. Flour the pan.

Place eggs and sugar in mixing bowl. Set over simmering water, whisking until the sugar dissolves and the mixture is barely lukewarm, about 100 degrees. Remove from heat. Beat on high speed until tripled in volume, about 4 minutes.

Sift together flour, cocoa powder and baking soda in a bowl. Gradually add to the egg mixture, beating on lowest speed until not quite incorporated. Add melted butter and vanilla, beat for another minute, until barely mixed.

Pour at once into the prepared pan, smooth the top with a rubber spatula. Tap the pan gently on the counter to release air bubbles. Bake in lower third of the oven until the cake begins to pull away from the sides and the center feels moist and spongy, not liquid when pressed (do not open the oven until almost baked), approximately 25 to 30 minutes.

Cool on a rack for 5 to 10 minutes. Run a thin knife around the pan to release the cake, then remove the side. Invert cake onto a rack, remove the bottom, then the paper. Cool completely.

Cut the cake into 2 equal layers with a long serrated knife. Wrap and freeze one layer for future cake making. Set one layer, cut side up, back in the springform pan on a round of wax paper. Paint evenly with raspberry syrup. Scoop the chocolate cream onto the cake, smooth with a spatula. Chill for at least 4 hours.

Final assembly: run a knife around rim of the pan, then carefully remove side. Grate extra bittersweet chocolate on the medium holes of a standing grater. Press gently onto the side of the cake to coat evenly. Sift cocoa powder over top. In a bowl, whisk together cream, powdered sugar and vanilla, until light and thick. Serve cake with a dollop of whipped cream.

RASPBERRY SYRUP

4 tablespoons raspberry preserves, seedless
1/4 cup sugar
1/4 cup water
1/4 cup dark rum or raspberry liqueur

Combine sugar, preserves and water in a small sauce pan, bring to a boil, stirring constantly. Remove from heat and stir in rum.

CHOCOLATE CREAM

1 square Bakers chocolate
9 ounces bittersweet chocolate, with 50% cocoa butter content
2 cups heavy or whipping cream
1/4 cup powdered sugar
2 teaspoons chocolate flavoring
2 egg yolks

Break the chocolate into small pieces and set in a bowl over hot, but not simmering water. When barely melted, remove from heat. Chocolate should be only about body temperature. Whip 1 2/3 cups cream until thickened and fluffy, but not firm enough to mound. Add 1/4 cup powdered sugar and chocolate flavoring, mixture should be slightly liquid. In a separate bowl blend together remaining 1/3 cup cream and egg yolks. Pour this into the chocolate all at once, then stir lightly but rapidly with a rubber spatula to blend. Pour in whipped cream and blend gently. Use immediately.

Toula Patsalis
Kitchen Glamour
Member of the International Association of Culinary Professionals
Detroit, Michigan

CHOCOLATE RASPBERRY ALMOND TORTE

The flavors of raspberries and chocolate complement each other in this sinfully rich dessert. Decorate the torte with chocolate and lemon leaves. Make chocolate leaves by coating one side of a lemon leaf with melted chocolate, chilling and then carefully removing the leaf. Lemon leaves are available from a florist, or if not available use ficus leaves.

½ cup blanched almonds, toasted lightly
2 ounces unsweetened chocolate
2 tablespoons unsalted butter
2 large eggs
1 cup sugar
1 tablespoon framboise or raspberry brandy
¾ cup flour
1 teaspoon double acting baking powder
¼ teaspoon salt
1 cup raspberries
Glaze
Ganache
lemon leaves

---

serves 8

Preheat oven to 350 degrees. Butter an 8½ inch springform pan.

In a food processor chop almonds, scraping the bowl occasionally, for 5 minutes, or until the consistency of nut butter, reserve. In a bowl set over barely simmering water melt the chocolate and butter, stirring occasionally. When melted, remove the bowl from the heat.

In the large bowl of an electric mixer, beat the eggs until they are pale. Continue beating and begin adding the sugar gradually, until mixture is very thick and pale. Beat in chocolate mixture, framboise, and reserved almond butter, until it is well blended. Into the batter, sift together the flour, baking powder and salt, and continue beating until well blended. Gently fold in 1 cup of raspberries.

Turn the mixture into the prepared pan, spreading it evenly and smoothing the top. Bake torte in the middle of the oven for 40 to 45 minutes, or until a skewer comes out clean. Let the torte cool on a rack and remove the side of the pan.

Place a sheet of wax paper on top of a rack. Invert the torte onto the rack, remove the bottom of the pan, and spread the glaze on the top and side of the torte. Let the torte stand at room temperature for 2 hours or chill for 30 minutes, until glaze is set. The torte may be prepared up to this point 1 day in advance and kept on the rack, covered with an inverted bowl, at room temperature.

Pour Ganache over the torte, smoothing with a spatula and letting the excess drip down the side. Let torte stand for 1 hour, or until the Ganache is set. Transfer torte carefully to a serving plate, garnish with additional raspberries and lemon leaves. Serve the remaining raspberries, garnished with lemon leaves, separately.

GLAZE

1/3 cup raspberry jam with the seeds
1 tablespoon sugar

In a heavy sauce pan combine jam and sugar. Bring the mixture to a boil while stirring. Continue boiling and stirring for 3 minutes. Force the mixture through a fine sieve into a small bowl, pressing hard on the seeds. Discard seeds.

GANACHE

1/4 cup heavy cream
6 ounces fine quality bittersweet chocolate, chopped

In a small, heavy sauce pan bring cream to a boil, remove pan from heat, and add chocolate. Stir until smooth, and cool for 3 minutes.

Jane Montant
Editor in Chief, GOURMET magazine
New York, New York

DELIGHTFUL STRAWBERRY NUT CAKE

Strawberry lovers will enjoy this cake, rich with the fruit's tantalizing flavor. This cake proved to be a favorite of television viewers when demonstrated by Barbara McKay on WBTV Channel 3 in Charlotte, North Carolina.

---

1 cup oil
4 eggs
½ cup milk
3 ounce package strawberry gelatin
1½ cups frozen strawberries, thawed
1 yellow cake mix (2 layer package)
1½ cups chopped pecans
1½ cups coconut
1 pound powdered sugar
½ cup margarine, softened

---

serves 12

Preheat oven to 350 degrees. Grease and flour two 9 inch cake pans.

Combine oil, eggs and milk in mixer bowl, mix well. Add gelatin, 1 cup strawberries and cake mix. Beat until smooth. Gently fold in 1 cup pecans and 1 cup coconut. Spoon into prepared cake pans. Bake for 20 minutes. Cool on wire rack.

For frosting, combine powdered sugar, margarine, remaining strawberries, pecans and coconut in a bowl, mix well. Spread between layers, and over the top and sides of cake.

BARBARA MCKAY
Charlotte, North Carolina

MARILYN'S BLUEBERRY KUCHEN

The perfect complement for summer berries, this easy yet delicious cake can be served plain, with a dollop of whipped cream or with ice cream.

---

1 cup flour
1/8 teaspoon salt
2 tablespoons sugar
1/2 cup butter
1 tablespoon white vinegar
5 cups fresh blueberries
2 tablespoons flour
2/3 cup sugar
1/8 teaspoon cinnamon

---

serves 6

Preheat oven to 400 degrees.

Mix together 1 cup flour, salt and 2 tablespoons sugar. Cut in butter until crumbly. Sprinkle with vinegar. Shape into a ball with floured hands. In a 9 inch springform pan, press dough to approximately 1/4 inch thickness on bottom and thinner on sides. Bring sides up 1 inch high.

Pour 3 cups blueberries over crust in pan. Mix 2 tablespoons flour with 2/3 cup sugar and cinnamon. Sprinkle over blueberries. Bake on lowest rack 50 to 60 minutes. Filling should be bubbling, and the crust brown. Remove to cooling rack. Pour remaining 2 cups berries on top, cool. When cool, remove from springform pan.

Paula Finkle
Zachman & Associates
Miami, Florida

SUNSHINE CAKE

The Watts Tea Shop replaced the Cooks Tea Shop, which was founded in 1901 by the "Cook Sisters". The Sunshine Cake is one of their original recipes and is still a favorite at the tea shop.

---

9 eggs
1/4 cup water
1 teaspoon vanilla
1 cup sugar
1 cup cake flour, sifted three times
1 teaspoon cream of tartar
1/4 teaspoon salt
French Custard Filling
Boiled Frosting
grated orange rind

---

serves 16

Preheat oven to 350 degrees.

Separate eggs into yolks and whites, reserve. Beat yolks, water, vanilla and 1/2 cup sugar together until light and fluffy. Add flour in several additions. In a separate bowl, whip egg whites with cream of tartar and salt until soft peaks form. Add 1/2 cup sugar to the egg whites and beat until stiff. Fold into batter. Bake in ungreased tube pan for 45 minutes. Let cool thoroughly.

Carefully cut cake into three layers, and fill with French Custard Filling. Cover top and sides of the three layer cake with Boiled Frosting. Grate the rind of a large orange over top.

FRENCH CUSTARD FILLING

4 egg yolks, beaten
3/4 cup sifted powdered sugar
3/4 cup milk
1 teaspoon vanilla
1 cup butter

Combine yolks, powdered sugar and milk in double boiler and cook until custard coats stirring spoon and begins to thicken. Cool. Add vanilla. Cream butter thoroughly, add to custard slowly while beating mixture. Spread between cake layers.

BOILED FROSTING

1/2 cup water
1 1/3 cups sugar
pinch of salt
3 egg whites
1 teaspoon vanilla

Boil water, sugar and pinch of salt until syrup spins a thread. Beat egg whites until soft peaks form. Pour hot syrup into beaten egg whites very slowly. Beat constantly in electric mixer until frosting stands in stiff peaks and is of spreading consistency. Add vanilla.

WATTS TEA SHOP
George Watts and Son, Inc.
Milwaukee, Wisconsin

MY FAVORITE CAKE

This cake is delightful when accompanied with fresh berries and a dollop of whipped cream. Ellen dedicated her favorite cake to Ron, "whose warmth and charm we will always remember."

---

6 eggs
1½ cups sweet butter
3 cups sugar
3 cups flour
¼ teaspoon baking soda
1 cup sour cream
2 teaspoons vanilla
sugar

---

serves 16

Preheat oven to 325 degrees. Grease and flour a 10 inch tube pan.

Separate eggs into yolks and whites, beat yolks. Cream butter with sugar, mix in yolks. Sift flour with baking soda and add alternately with sour cream to batter. Stir in vanilla. In separate bowl, beat egg whites until stiff. Fold into batter carefully, but thoroughly. Pour batter into prepared pan. Bake for 1½ hours or slightly less. Let stand 10 minutes in pan, then turn upside down on a rack. Sprinkle top with a little sugar while still warm. Serve in thin wedges.

ELLEN GORDON
Brookline, Massachusetts

BROWNIES OF DEATH

After skiing down the mountain slopes skiers often have a craving for chocolate. It's appropriate this "brownie to die for" originated in Aspen. Espresso powder and white chocolate chips can be found in select supermarkets and specialty stores.

½ cup butter
½ cup semisweet chocolate
1 tablespoon espresso powder
4 eggs, room temperature
½ teaspoon salt
2 cups sugar
1 cup flour, sifted
1 cup white chocolate chips
powdered sugar

---

makes 24 brownies

Preheat oven to 350 degrees. Grease a 9x13 inch bake pan.

Melt butter and chocolate in a heavy sauce pan or double boiler. Dissolve espresso powder in chocolate mixture, cool. Beat eggs and salt until foamy.

Gradually add sugar. Combine cooled chocolate mixture with eggs and sugar. Fold in flour and chocolate chips. Pour into prepared pan and bake for approximately 25 minutes. When brownies cool, dust with powdered sugar.

Sally Jo Mullen
Les Chefs D'Aspen
Member of the International Association of Culinary Professionals
Aspen, Colorado

CALIFORNIA TOFFEE BUTTER CRUNCH

This recipe can easily be doubled by doubling all the ingredients, except the chocolate bars. Increase this amount to 30 chocolate bars.

1½ cups roasted, salted almonds
12 Hershey milk chocolate bars (1.65 ounces)
1 cup sweet butter
1⅓ cups sugar
1 tablespoon light corn syrup
3 tablespoons water

---

makes 36 pieces

Butter a 9x13 inch bake pan. Coarsely chop half the nuts and set aside. Finely chop the remaining nuts and sprinkle buttered pan with one half of the finely chopped nuts. Cover with six chocolate bars. In a large heavy sauce pan melt butter, then add sugar, corn syrup and water. Using a candy thermometer, cook over medium heat, stirring occasionally, to 300 degrees. Quickly stir in the coarsely chopped nuts and pour over chocolate bars. Immediately cover with remaining chocolate bars and sprinkle top with rest of finely chopped nuts. Lay a large sheet of wax paper across top of pan and press gently so nuts will adhere. Chill and break into pieces. Can be frozen.

Arlene Harris
The Chef's Catalog
Northbrook, Illinois

GRAMMA "J's" PRALINES

This recipe is quick, easy, and takes less than 30 minutes from start to finish. Vary this recipe by substituting your favorite nuts.

---

graham crackers
1 cup butter
1 cup packed brown sugar
¼ teaspoon cream of tartar
½ cup or more chopped walnuts

Preheat oven to 325 degrees. Break graham crackers apart. Line the bottom of a 1x1x18 inch cookie sheet with the graham crackers.

Put butter, sugar and cream of tartar in sauce pan and stir. Bring to a full rolling boil, add nuts and bring to a boil again, continue stirring until sugar and butter are thoroughly blended. Pour caramel coating over graham crackers and cover completely. Bake for 13 minutes. Remove from oven and cool 3 minutes. Remove individual crackers with spatula and place on aluminum foil to finish cooling.

Betty Feeney
Betty Feeney's, Ltd.
Boise, Idaho

JUMBLES

This recipe originated in Germany and has been in the Kahle family for over 100 years. The cookies are wonderful served with tea.

---

2 cups sugar
1 cup butter
1 teaspoon salt
1 teaspoon vanilla
2 eggs
3 cups flour
3 to 4 egg whites, beaten stiff
3 tablespoons sugar
1 tablespoon plus 2 teaspoons cinnamon
1 tablespoon nutmeg

---

yields 36 cookies

Preheat oven to 375 degrees. Grease cookie sheets.

Cream together sugar and butter. Add salt, vanilla, whole eggs and mix well. Add flour and mix thoroughly. Shape into 1 inch balls, approximately the size of a walnut. Place on cookie sheet and flatten with bottom of a glass, about 1/8 inch thick.

Beat egg whites until stiff. Spread one tablespoon of stiffened egg whites on top of each cookie.

Mix sugar, cinnamon and nutmeg together, then sprinkle a pinch over each jumble. Bake 8 to 10 minutes until light golden brown around edges. Grease cookie sheet before each additional baking.

SARAH AND ROSEMARY KAHLE
Perrysburg, Ohio

TEXAS GOLD BARS

For holidays, substitute candied cherries and pineapple for the chocolate chips.

---

1 yellow cake mix (2 layer package)
3 eggs
½ cup butter
1 pound powdered sugar
8 ounces cream cheese
1 teaspoon vanilla
1 cup chopped pecans
1 cup mini chocolate chips

Preheat oven to 350 degrees. Butter a 9x13 inch baking pan.

Mix together cake mix, 1 egg and butter. Pat into bottom of prepared pan. Combine 2 eggs, powdered sugar, cream cheese, vanilla, nuts and chips, and pour over top of first layer. Bake 50 to 60 minutes. Cool for 10 minutes, then cut into 1 inch bars.

CAROLYN SALAS
Kitchen Stuff
Lufkin, Texas

WHITE CHOCOLATE & PECAN STUDDED BROWNIES

These brownies were created as a special treat that could be mailed to Betty's son in college. We recommend them for all occasions - a picnic, shipping to a chocoholic, or simply to enjoy yourself. In an air tight container, they will last four to five days.

---

3 ounces unsweetened chocolate, broken into small pieces
3/4 cup unsalted butter, softened slightly
3/4 cup sugar
3/4 cup firmly packed light brown sugar
3 eggs
3/4 cup flour
6 ounces white chocolate, cut into 1/2 inch pieces
1 cup coarsely chopped pecans
powdered sugar

---

yields 32 brownies

Preheat oven to 350 degrees. Butter and flour a 9x13 inch bakepan. Cut a sheet of aluminum foil to fit bottom of pan. Butter and flour foil and shake off excess. Place, buttered side up, in pan.

In top of a double boiler set over simmering water, melt unsweetened chocolate, stirring until chocolate is smooth and shiny. Remove from heat and set aside.

Cream butter with a mixer set on medium speed. Gradually add sugars. On slow speed, pour in melted chocolate. Add eggs, one at a time, and mix only until incorporated. Add flour. Remove bowl from mixer and stir in white chocolate pieces, and pecans with a spatula or wooden spoon.

Pour brownie mixture into prepared pan and using a spatula, spread evenly. Bake brownies on center shelf until a toothpick inserted in the middle comes out almost clean (there might be a few specks of chocolate on it), about 20 to 25 minutes. Remove and cool to room temperature.

When cool, invert the brownies onto a work surface and peel off foil. Invert again and sprinkle lightly with powdered sugar.

BETTY ROSBOTTOM
La Belle Pomme Cooking School at Lazarus, Columbus, Ohio
Member of the International Association of Culinary Professionals
Recipe courtesy of LOS ANGELES TIMES syndicate

APPLE TART TARTAN

The Apple Tart Tartan is baked with the crust on top for perfect browning, then inverted onto a platter so the apples are on top. The Pâté Brisée, or pastry dough, can also be used for pies and quiches.

---

8 large Granny Smith apples, peeled, cored, quartered
juice of 1 lemon
1½ cups sugar
½ cup butter, cut into large pieces
1 recipe Pâté Brisée

---

16 slices

Preheat oven to 425 degrees.

Cut each apple quarter into 4 slices. Sprinkle with lemon juice and reserve.

Place sugar in a 3 quart Calphalon sauté pan. Heat on medium heat until sugar melts and becomes golden brown. Be careful not to burn sugar. Add ½ cup butter and stir until melted. Add apples and stir to coat slices with caramel. Bring to a simmer and cook until apples are tender and moisture has evaporated.

Lightly butter a 14 inch Calphalon pizza pan. Spread caramelized apples in the pan. Roll out dough on a lightly floured surface to form a 14 inch circle. Place on top of apple mixture.

Put on top oven rack and bake until crust is golden and crisp, approximately 20 minutes. Remove, let set briefly and turn over onto a large tray. Scrape any apples out of the pizza pan and smooth over top of tart. Serve with whipped cream.

PÂTÉ BRISÉE

---

2 cups flour
1 cup butter, cold, cut into large dice
2 teaspoons lemon juice
1½ teaspoons lemon zest
5 to 6 tablespoons ice cold water

---

makes one 14 inch or two 10 inch crusts

Place flour in a food processor. Add 1 cup cold butter and process to a fine crumb. Add lemon juice and zest. Process to combine. Slowly add cold water and process until dough begins to stick together, more or less water may be needed. Remove dough and form into ball. Wrap with plastic wrap and refrigerate until ready to use.

Carol Cole Caldwell
Food Consultant
New York, New York

SOUR CREAM APPLE PIE

We tested this recipe the week before Thanksgiving and found that many of the tasters served it for their own Thanksgiving dinners. Use your own favorite pie crust or try our Sweet Crust for this non-traditional apple pie.

---

2 eggs
1/2 cup sugar
1 cup sour cream
1 1/2 tablespoons flour
1/2 teaspoon vanilla
1/4 teaspoon salt
4 medium to large tart apples, peeled, cored, thinly sliced
9 inch unbaked pie shell or 1 recipe for Sweet Crust
6 tablespoons brown sugar
1/2 cup flour
3 tablespoons butter or margarine, softened

---

serves 8

Preheat oven to 400 degrees.

In a medium bowl beat eggs lightly. Add sugar, sour cream, flour, vanilla and salt, mixing well. Add apples and toss until slices are thoroughly coated with mixture. Turn mixture into your favorite unbaked pie shell or use the Sweet Crust. Bake 30 minutes.

While pie is baking, make topping. In small bowl, combine brown sugar, flour and butter, mixing well until crumbly.

After 30 minutes remove pie from oven, and lower oven temperature to 350 degrees. Sprinkle topping evenly over pie and return to oven for 15 minutes.

LESTER GRIBETZ
Bloomingdale's
New York, New York

CASSATA PIE

6 eggs
1½ cups sugar
45 ounces ricotta cheese
1½ tablespoons vanilla
⅛ teaspoon salt
1 egg yolk
Sweet Crust

Preheat oven to 350 degrees.

Separate egg yolks and whites into two bowls. Whisk egg yolks and sugar until mixture is in a ribbon state. Add ricotta cheese, vanilla and salt to mixture. Mix thoroughly.

Whisk egg whites until soft peaks form. Fold egg whites into egg yolk mixture. Set aside.

Flour pastry cloth and rolling pin. Roll Sweet Crust dough to fit a large pie pan. Place dough in pie pan, trim and flute edges. Pour filling into pie shell. Beat egg yolk, then dribble over the top of filling and gently spread to glaze the surface.

Bake for 1 hour or until toothpick inserted into middle comes out clean. Serve chilled.

SWEET CRUST

2 cups flour
1 teaspoon salt
½ cup Crisco, frozen
½ cup butter, frozen
½ cup sugar
3 to 5 tablespoons ice water

Using a food processor fitted with a metal knife attachment, blend flour and salt. Separately, cut up shortening and butter into small pieces, then evenly distribute in processor bowl. Pulse processor several times until mixture is in pea-size pieces.

Sprinkle with one tablespoon water and pulse. Check dough. Mixture should hold together when pinched. Repeat with each tablespoon of water until mixture is correct consistency. Form dough into a ball, wrap in wax paper, and refrigerate for ½ hour.

Paul Angelo LoGiudice
Culinary Events Specialist
Commercial Aluminum Cookware Company

RICE TART
WITH FRESH FRUIT

Arborio is Italian short grain rice. Use your favorite fruit such as pears, peaches, apricots, fresh berries, or whatever is in season. A mixture of fruit is also delicious.

2/3 recipe Sugar Dough
1/2 cup Arborio rice
2 cups milk
zest of 2 oranges
1 vanilla bean, split and scraped
1/2 cup sugar
7 tablespoons unsalted butter, softened
4 egg yolks
1/2 cup Grand Marnier
2 cups heavy cream, lightly whipped
1 cup poached sliced fruit
1/4 cup sugar plus extra as needed

Preheat oven to 350 degrees. Line baking sheet with parchment paper.

On a floured surface, roll sugar dough about 3/8 inch thick. Take the dough and line six or eight 4x1/2 inch flan rings, or one 8 inch pie tin or flan ring with the dough. Place rings on the parchment covered baking sheet. Place coffee filters or parchment paper over dough and weight with pie weights or dried beans. Bake for about 20 to 25 minutes, or until tart shells are golden brown. Remove from oven and let cool. Remove pie weights and paper. Chill tart shells.

Place rice in a sauce pan and add just enough water to cover. Bring rice to a boil and cook over moderate heat for 2 minutes, drain rice. In an ovenproof sauce pan, add milk, orange zest, vanilla bean and sugar. Add rice to the sauce pan, stir, and bring to a boil. When boiling, cover the pan, and place in oven for about 30 minutes, or until rice is cooked and liquid is absorbed.

While rice is cooking, cream soft butter. Add egg yolks, one at time, mixing well until incorporated. The mixture should be smooth and satiny.

When rice is done remove pan from oven and transfer to a burner. Whisk in the egg/butter mixture over low heat until mixture has thickened. Remove vanilla bean. Stir in Grand Marnier and cool. Fold in lightly whipped cream and chill until nearly set.

Line bottom of chilled tart shells with fruit. Pour rice mixture into shell over fruit, smooth the tops and chill until set, about 30 minutes.

Before serving, caramelize the tops of the tarts by sprinkling a tablespoon of sugar on each tart (about 1/4 cup sugar for a large tart). Place under a hot broiler or use a small blow torch. Take care to brown only the sugar, not burn tarts. Remove the rings. Serve on individual plates with a sauce made from a puree of the same fruit in the tart.

SUGAR DOUGH

This dough may also be made in a food processor, but make half a batch at a time for best results.

---

2 cups unsalted butter, slightly softened
3 1/3 cups pastry flour
3 1/3 cups all-purpose flour
pinch of salt
3/4 cup sugar
3 egg yolks
2 tablespoons heavy cream

---

yields 2 1/2 pounds

Cut butter into large pieces and place pieces in the bowl of an electric mixer fitted with a paddle or dough hook. Add the pastry and all-purpose flour, salt and sugar. Mix on low speed until butter is evenly distributed throughout the flour. Add egg yolks and cream. Continue to mix on low speed until the dough pulls away from the sides of the bowl.

Remove dough and divide it into 2 pieces. Flatten each piece into a 6 inch round. Wrap in plastic and chill for at least 2 hours or overnight. Use as needed. The dough will remain fresh for 2 to 3 days in the refrigerator, or wrap securely in plastic, not foil, and it will keep frozen 2 to 3 months.

WOLFGANG PUCK
Spago California Cuisine, Chinois, and Eureka restaurants
Author of THE WOLFGANG PUCK COOKBOOK
Los Angeles, California

CHOCOLATE CHESS PIE

This pie has a wonderful flavor and has a crunchy texture on top after it is baked. Test pie with a cake tester to be sure it is set before removing from oven.

---

4 egg yolks
1 whole egg, slightly beaten
1½ cups sugar
½ cup boiling water
½ cup melted butter
1 teaspoon vanilla
¼ cup cocoa
1 unbaked pie crust

---

serves 6-8

Preheat oven to 350 degrees.

Beat egg yolks and egg with sugar. Bring water and butter to boil in 1½ quart sauce pan, mix in vanilla and cocoa. Cool, then add to egg mixture. Pour into crust. Bake on lowest rack in oven until set, about 30 to 40 minutes. If pie gets too brown, reduce oven temperature.

SUE SIMS
The Pan-Tree
International Association of Culinary Professionals
San Angelo, Texas

1979

FROZEN AVOCADO & LIME PIE
WITH LIME WHIPPED CREAM

13 ounce package coconut macaroons, crushed
1/2 cup unsalted butter, melted
3 ripe avocados
1 teaspoon lime zest, (without bitter white pith)
juice of 6 limes
1/2 cup granulated sugar
1 cup sweetened condensed milk
2 eggs, separated
whipped cream
lime zest and juice

Combine macaroons and butter in a bowl, blend well. Press into a 10 inch pie pan. Chill in freezer.

Pit avocados and scoop out flesh. Puree in food processor until smooth. Add zest, lime juice, sugar, condensed milk and egg yolks. Blend until smooth. Transfer to bowl.

In a clean bowl, whip egg whites until stiff but not dry. Fold whites into puree in three parts, incorporating each before adding more. Pour into pie shell. Smooth out top and freeze. Cover when frozen.

Thaw 15 minutes in refrigerator before serving. Serve with whipped cream flavored with lime zest and juice.

pictured
venison with juniper & port sauce, 122

marilyn's blueberry kuchen, 185
orange slices in champagne-ginger sauce, 162
my favorite cake, 188
chilled lemon soufflé with warm carmel sauce, 212
apple tart tartan, 195
chocolate raspberry almond torte, 182

polenta pudding with fresh blackberry compote, 222

PHILIPPE JEANTY
Chef de Cuisine, Domaine Chandon restaurant, Napa Valley
Yountville, California

PEANUT BUTTER PIE

A creative use for the great American favorite - peanut butter. Substitute a regular, or a chocolate wafer crushed crust for variety. Drizzle chocolate over the top, or garnish with chocolate shavings for a festive touch.

---

2 cups milk
½ cup sugar
1 heaping tablespoon cornstarch
½ teaspoon salt
3 egg yolks
½ cup peanut butter
graham cracker crust
whipped cream

---

serves 8

Scald 2 cups milk in a 1 quart sauce pan. Mix sugar, cornstarch and salt in a 2½ quart sauce pan. Beat 3 egg yolks and add to mixture in 2½ quart sauce pan. Mix well. Slowly add the scalded milk to egg mixture. Cook over low heat until thick, stirring constantly. Stir in peanut butter until smooth. Pour into graham cracker crust. Cover with whipped cream sweetened to cook's taste. Chill for at least 4 hours. Garnish with chopped peanuts before serving.

Susan Heine
Island Kitchen
Marco Island, Florida

APPLE BLUEBERRY COBBLER

This different version of an American favorite blends the flavor of blueberries with apples. Can be served warm with vanilla ice cream or whipping cream.

---

8 cups apple slices, peeled, cored
2 cups fresh or frozen blueberries, thawed, drained
1 cup sugar
½ teaspoon cinnamon
¼ teaspoon nutmeg
1 cup flour
⅓ cup butter, melted then cooled
1 egg
1 teaspoon baking powder
¾ teaspoon salt

---

serves 8

Preheat oven to 350 degrees. Grease a 9x13 inch bake pan.

Mix apples and blueberries together and pour into prepared pan. Combine ½ cup sugar, cinnamon and nutmeg, sprinkle over apples and blueberries.

In a bowl mix the remaining ½ cup sugar, flour, butter, egg, baking powder and salt. Batter will be stiff. Drop by spoonfuls on top of apple mixture. Bake for 1 hour.

CAREY HEWITT
The Cupboard
Fort Collins, Colorado

CAROLYN'S BREAD PUDDING
WITH BOURBON SAUCE

2 teaspoons butter, softened
1½ cups day old French or Italian white bread
1 quart milk
3 eggs
2 cups sugar
2 teaspoons vanilla
½ cup seedless golden raisins
½ cup roasted walnut pieces
½ cup sugar
¼ cup butter
½ cup whipping cream
Bourbon Sauce

Preheat oven to 350 degrees. Butter a heavy terrine.

Break bread into pieces in a large bowl and pour milk over the bread. When bread has absorbed milk, crumble into small bits.

Beat eggs with sugar until light and thick. Add vanilla, then pour egg mixture over bread and mix together. Stir in raisins and walnuts and pour into prepared terrine.

Place terrine in a large pan filled with hot water to come up halfway on terrine. Bake for approximately 45 minutes or until firm.

Remove from oven and sprinkle sugar over top of pudding. Dot with butter and pour cream over the top. Return to oven, increase heat to 425 degrees and bake until lightly browned, and sugar is caramelized. Serve with hot Bourbon Sauce.

BOURBON SAUCE

3 egg yolks
1/2 cup sugar
2 teaspoons cornstarch
1 1/2 cups milk
1/2 cup butter
1 teaspoon vanilla
1 1/2 ounces brandy
1/2 cup bourbon

Beat together egg yolks and sugar until light and thick. Dissolve cornstarch in 3 tablespoons of milk. Heat remaining milk and butter until boiling. Add a small amount of the hot milk and butter to the egg yolk mixture then mix this into the hot milk. Whip in cornstarch mixture. Remove from heat and stir in vanilla, brandy and bourbon. Serve hot over bread pudding.

Carolyn Buster
The Cottage restaurant
Member of the International Association of Culinary Professionals
Calumet City, Illinois

BARACK GOMBOC

HUNGARIAN APRICOT DUMPLINGS

Yuval Zaliouk is the former Conductor of the Toledo Symphony and is now a guest conductor at orchestras around the world. Yuval's company, YZ Enterprises, makes another family recipe, Almondina Biscuits, which are sold at many gourmet stores.

---

8 ounces cream cheese
1 cup flour plus extra as needed
1 egg
fresh or dried (soaked) apricots
½ cup butter
3 tablespoons bread crumbs
1 teaspoon cinnamon mixed with 3 tablespoons granulated sugar

---

Mix cheese, flour and egg into a dough. Knead, adding a little flour if necessary, until dough is smooth. Divide dough into small balls, flatten to small rounds, about 3 inch in diameter and ¼ inch thick. Put half an apricot in the middle, fold over and seal.

Gently put dumplings into boiling water. Boil for 10 minutes until dumplings float. Remove and set aside. Up to this point, the recipe can be prepared in advance.

Just before serving, melt butter in frying pan. Add bread crumbs to pan. Put dumplings in pan, turning to coat with bread crumbs. Serve warm in individual dishes. Sprinkle with cinnamon sugar.

YUVAL ZALIOUK
YZ Enterprises, Inc.
Maumee, Ohio

COLD CHESTNUT SOUFFLÉ

The subtle rum flavor of this soufflé will take the chill off those cold fall and winter days. An excellent dessert for entertaining since it can be prepared a day in advance.

---

4 eggs
3 egg yolks
½ cup sugar
2 tablespoons gelatin
¼ cup dark rum
1 cup sweetened canned chestnut puree
1 cup heavy cream, stiffly beaten
favorite chocolate sauce
½ cup heavy cream

---

serves 9

Butter a 6 inch band of wax paper and tie around a ¾ quart buttered soufflé dish to form a standing collar.

Combine eggs, egg yolks and sugar in a mixing bowl. Beat for about 15 minutes, or until thick and pale in color. Soften gelatin in dark rum and dissolve over hot water. Beat gelatin and rum mixture quickly into beaten eggs. Combine with chestnut puree, and mix well. Fold in 1 cup stiffly beaten heavy cream. Fill the prepared dish with the soufflé mixture and chill until set, approximately 30 minutes to an hour.

Before serving, carefully remove paper collar. Beat ½ cup heavy cream and press through a pastry bag fitted with a fluted tube. Decorate top of soufflé with rosettes.

Serve with favorite chocolate sauce mixed with whipped cream.

Susan Reams
Perrysburg, Ohio

CHILLED LEMON SOUFFLÉ
WITH WARM CARAMEL SAUCE

Gordon Sinclair receives rave reviews when he serves this refreshing dessert in his restaurant. Don't let the length of this recipe intimidate you - it is not difficult and well worth the effort.

1¼ cups sugar
pinch of cream of tartar
¾ cup water
6 tablespoons lemon juice
1¾ cups milk
grated zest of 2 lemons
5 egg yolks
3 tablespoons cornstarch
3 tablespoons sugar
7 egg whites
4 tablespoons sugar
pinch of cream of tartar

---

serves 8

Preheat oven to 375 degrees. Prepare a 2½ quart metal charlotte mold by combining 1¼ cups sugar, cream of tartar and water in a sauce pan. Heat on high until golden brown. Carefully pour into mold and rotate to cover entire interior surface, cool. Sugar may crack but this has no effect on the soufflé.

Pour lemon juice in a large bowl, reserve. Heat milk in a sauce pan. Mix together zest, yolks, cornstarch and 3 tablespoons sugar and temper into heated milk. Stir mixture constantly. It will clump as it approaches the boiling point, continue stirring and clumps will disappear. Once mixture boils continue stirring for 1½ minutes.

Pour mixture into bowl with the lemon juice and stir thoroughly, reserve. In a bowl whip egg whites with 4 tablespoons sugar and a pinch of cream of tartar, until soft peaks form. Fold egg whites into warm lemon mixture using a spatula. Pour mixture into prepared charlotte mold.

Smooth top and place mold in a water bath. Bake for 1¼ hours until top is golden. Refrigerate overnight and unmold. Serve with Warm Caramel Sauce.

WARM CARAMEL SAUCE

6 tablespoons butter
2¼ cups sugar
2 cups heavy cream

Melt butter in a sauce pan. Add sugar and stir until the sugar becomes a light golden color. Stir cream into the caramelized sugar. Boil to reduce enough to coat the spoon. Drizzle over soufflé servings.

Gordon A. Sinclair
Gordon's restaurant
Board Member of the American Institute of Wine and Food
Chicago, Illinois

DEEP DISH GINGERED PEACH COBBLER

14 tablespoons butter
1 teaspoon candied ginger
3/4 cup sugar
1/4 cup brown sugar
1/8 teaspoon nutmeg
1/2 teaspoon salt
5 cups peaches (6 peaches), peeled, sliced
1 1/2 cups flour
1 teaspoon baking soda
1/2 cup buttermilk
1 egg

serves 6

Preheat oven to 350 degrees.

In a Calphalon 2 quart sauteuse pan, melt 6 tablespoons of butter on low heat. Remove pan from heat.

In a food processor, fitted with the metal knife attachment, mix candied ginger, 1/4 cup sugar, brown sugar, nutmeg, and 1/4 teaspoon salt. Mix until ginger is completely cut into mixture.

Place peaches in a large bowl and toss with candied ginger mixture until coated. Pour peaches into the 2 quart sauteuse pan and combine with melted butter.

In a large bowl, mix flour, 1/2 cup sugar, baking soda and 1/4 teaspoon salt. Set aside.

Melt 8 tablespoons of butter in a 1 1/2 quart Calphalon sauce pan. Remove from heat and slowly whisk in buttermilk. Add the egg and beat into mixture. Pour liquid ingredients into dry ingredients and mix thoroughly. Spoon dough over peaches in sauteuse pan to make cobbled effect. Bake for 45 to 50 minutes. Cool for 15 minutes. Serve with vanilla ice cream.

Paul Angelo LoGiudice
Culinary Events Specialist
Commercial Aluminum Cookware Company

DEEP FRIED RASPBERRIES
WITH VANILLA SAUCE

raspberries or favorite fruit
2 cups flour
pinch of salt
pinch of sugar
1 bottle Coors Beer
5 egg whites
salad oil
cooking oil
cinnamon sugar

serves 4-6

In a mixing bowl, combine flour with a pinch of salt and sugar. Using a wire whisk, slowly add beer until mixture is a creamy consistency. In a separate bowl, beat egg whites until they form stiff peaks. Fold them into the batter. If you are not using the batter immediately, sprinkle the top with a very small amount of salad oil to keep a skin from forming on top. More beer can be added, if needed.

Heat 4 inches of oil in a deep pan. Dry each piece of fruit, dip in beer batter, and cook in hot oil until golden brown. Remove fruit from hot oil and drain on absorbent toweling. Roll deep fried fruit in cinnamon sugar until evenly coated. Serve on a bed of Vanilla Sauce. Vary the recipe by using bananas, pears, apples or grapes..

VANILLA SAUCE

4 cups half and half
½ vanilla bean
sugar
5 egg yolks

Combine half and half, vanilla bean, and sugar to taste. Bring to a boil in a double boiler. Place five egg yolks in a mixing bowl and beat thoroughly with a wire whisk.

Slowly whisk boiling cream mixture into egg yolks. To help keep the sauce from curdling, place the mixing bowl in a hot bath. Remove vanilla bean before serving.

Nancy Gilbert
A Short Story
Broadmoor Hotel
Colorado Springs, Colorado

ESPRESSO & MASCARPONE ICE CREAM SANDWICH

WITH A CRUNCHY PEANUT BUTTER LAYER AND BITTERSWEET CHOCOLATE SAUCE

Espresso Ice Cream
Mascarpone Ice Cream
Peanut Butter Layer
Cookie Crust
Bittersweet Chocolate Sauce
60 espresso beans

---

makes 6 sandwiches

Make Espresso and Mascarpone Ice Creams using the Basic Ice Cream Sauce recipe. Make Peanut Butter Layer and Cookie Crust. Before asembling sandwiches and serving, make Bittersweet Chocolate Sauce.

Very gently, line up 6 Cookie Crust circles. Fill 3 pastry bags ready with Espresso Ice Cream, Peanut Butter Layer, and Mascarpone Ice Cream.

Pipe a layer of Espresso Ice Cream on top of circle, then a layer of Peanut Butter Layer and finish with a layer of Mascarpone Ice Cream. Place another cookie crust circle on top and press gently to bind the sandwich. Place onto a plate. Repeat with remaining circles. Serve each sandwich with a spoonful of warm Bittersweet Chocolate Sauce and sprinkle a few espresso beans for garnish.

BASIC ICE CREAM SAUCE

1 quart half and half
15 egg yolks
1 cup sugar
1 vanilla bean, split

Yields 2 batches

Heat half and half in a sauce pan. In a separate heavy sauce pan, whisk egg yolks and add sugar a little at a time. Beat until pale and thick. In a slow steady stream, mix in heated half and half. Add vanilla bean. Slowly stir mixture over low heat until it thickens and coats the back of a wooden spoon. Remove from heat. Divide into two batches.

ESPRESSO ICE CREAM

1 batch Basic Ice Cream Sauce
2 double espressos, reduced by half

Combine ingredients and mix well. Bring to room temperature. Freeze in ice cream maker according to directions.

MASCARPONE ICE CREAM

1 batch Basic Ice Cream Sauce
1½ cups mascarpone cheese

Heat one batch of Basic Ice Cream Sauce. Add cheese and heat over low heat until cheese is melted and incorporated. Remove from heat and bring to room temperature. Freeze in ice cream maker according to directions. Do not overfreeze.

PEANUT BUTTER LAYER

1 cup light corn syrup
$^{3}/_{4}$ cup crunchy peanut butter, room temperature
2 tablespoons sweet butter
2 eggs at room temperature, lightly beaten
1 teaspoon vanilla extract

In a sauce pan, combine corn syrup and 4 tablespoons of water. Bring to a boil over medium heat and cook 5 minutes. Using a whisk, beat in the peanut butter until fairly smooth. Add butter and stir until melted. Remove sauce pan from heat. Slowly stir about 4 tablespoons of peanut butter mixture into beaten eggs, then add egg mixture to sauce pan. Cook over low heat, stirring constantly until the egg is cooked, about 2 minutes. Remove pan from heat and add vanilla. Refrigerate.

COOKIE CRUST

4 cups ground chocolate wafers
1 cup packed brown sugar
1 teaspoon ground cinnamon
1$^{1}/_{2}$ cups melted sweet butter

Combine all ingredients and mix well. Place a sheet of parchment paper on top of cookie sheet pan. Roll cookie mixture on top of paper to $^{1}/_{8}$ inch thick. Make circles 3$^{1}/_{4}$ inch diameter with a cookie cutter. Leave on pan and freeze.

BITTERSWEET CHOCOLATE SAUCE

1 cup cream
$^{1}/_{2}$ pound bittersweet chocolate, chopped
2 tablespoons sweet butter
1 teaspoon vanilla extract

In a heavy duty sauce pan, heat cream. Add rest of ingredients and blend well until smooth.

Philippe Jeanty
Chef de Cuisine
Domaine Chandon restaurant, Napa Valley
Yountville, California

NEW ORLEANS BREAD PUDDING
WITH HARD SAUCE

---

1 loaf stale French bread
5 eggs
1 cup sugar
1 tablespoon vanilla
1 cup pecans
1 cup raisins
1½ to 2 cups milk (depends on staleness of bread)
cinnamon
nutmeg

---

serves 8

Preheat oven to 350 degrees. Grease a 9x13 inch bake pan.

Break bread into pieces. In a bowl combine bread with eggs, sugar, vanilla, pecans and raisins. Slowly begin adding milk. Stop when bread falls apart when squeezed. Season to taste with cinnamon and nutmeg. Pour into prepared pan and bake for 45 minutes until baked through. Serve hot with Hard Sauce.

HARD SAUCE

½ cup butter
1 cup powdered sugar
bourbon to taste

Cream ingredients together.

Poppy Tooker
Walter Davis, Inc.
New Orleans, Louisiana

LEMON MERINGUE CRÊPES

Light and refreshing, the crêpe's delicate flavor is similar to lemon meringue pie. This is a perfect recipe for people who love to entertain, since the crêpes and lemon mixture can be made ahead and then assembled shortly before serving. Use this crêpe recipe or your own favorite.

---

4 eggs
⅔ cup sugar
⅓ cup freshly squeezed lemon juice
⅓ cup unsalted butter, cut into small pats
1 teaspoon grated lemon rind
¼ teaspoon cream of tartar
⅓ cup powdered sugar
8 crêpes

---

serves 4-6

For lemon filling, separate 4 eggs, reserve whites for meringue. Put 4 egg yolks into sauce pan, beat, add sugar and lemon juice, mix well. Cook over low heat, stirring constantly for approximately 10 to 12 minutes. The mixture should thicken, coating the back of a wooden spoon. Turn heat off at this point and add butter, a pat at a time, until each piece is blended into the mixture. Add lemon rind, cool completely.

To make meringue topping, beat reserved egg whites and cream of tartar in a mixing bowl until frothy. While beating, slowly add powdered sugar until whites are stiff.

Preheat broiler. Put ⅛ cup of lemon filling into each crêpe and roll up. Place in 13 inch au gratin. Continue with all crêpes, placing side by side in pan. Cover crêpes with meringue topping, using meringue to seal pan. Place in preheated broiler until the meringue is lightly browned, about 1 minute. Serve immediately.

CRÊPES

1 cup flour
pinch of salt
3 large eggs
1½ cups milk

yields 14-16 crêpes

Sift together flour and salt in mixing bowl. Add eggs and beat to combine. Slowly add milk, beating with each addition so batter is smooth. Batter should be heavy. Cover and reserve in refrigerator for about 1 hour to thicken.

Preheat crêpe pan on medium high heat until pan is hot. Lightly moisten a paper towel with oil, wipe inside of crêpe pan to lightly coat. Pour small ladle of batter, about ⅛ cup, into pan. Move pan in circular motion to coat bottom of pan. Pour off excess. Place back on heat and cook for about 1 minute. When edges appear golden, turn with a flexible spatula. Cook other side for about ½ minute and remove. Repeat process for remaining batter.

Layer crêpes in piles of 4 to 6, separated by wax paper or plastic wrap. Store extra crêpes in freezer.

JIM SALVESON
Los Angeles, California

POLENTA PUDDING

WITH FRESH BLACKBERRY COMPOTE AND "PETITE LIQUEUR" AND MASCARPONE CREAM

Polenta is cooked cornmeal; follow basic package directions to cook cornmeal. "Petite Liqueur," produced by Moet, is a combination of cognac and champagne. It is wonderful in the recipe, and to drink at the end of a perfect evening.

1½ cups sweet butter, softened
5 cups powdered sugar
¼ Tahitian vanilla bean, scrape inside
4 eggs
2 egg yolks
2 cups bread flour
1 cup polenta
Blackberry Compote
Mascarpone Cream

---

serves 6

Preheat oven to 325 degrees. Grease and flour a 12 inch cake pan.

In a mixing bowl, add butter, sugar and vanilla and beat with an electric mixer until smooth. One at a time, beat in the eggs and egg yolks. Fold in flour and polenta. Pour into a prepared cake pan. Bake 1 hour, 15 minutes. Unmold onto a wire rack and cool.

When cool, place cake in a large size cake pan. Pour Blackberry Compote and juices on top and around cake. Cover and soak overnight.

Just before serving, make Mascarpone Cream. Cut cake into slices, top with Mascarpone Cream and a few fresh blackberries. Add a few drops of "Petite Liqueur," pour some berry juice around the cake and garnish with a mint tip. Serve at room temperature.

BLACKBERRY COMPOTE

4 cups fresh blackberries
½ cup granulated sugar
¼ cup "Petite Liqueur"

Combine berries, sugar and "Petite Liqueur" in a sauce pan.

Cook uncovered until mixture is reduced to one half.

MASCARPONE CREAM

½ cup mascarpone cheese
1 cup whipping cream
3 tablespoons sugar

Combine ingredients and whip to a soft peak.

Philippe Jeanty
Chef de Cuisine, Domaine Chandon restaurant, Napa Valley
Yountville, California

PRUNE MOUSSE
WITH QUICK CUSTARD CREAM

12 ounces pitted prunes
1 cup water
2 envelopes unflavored gelatin
5 tablespoons lime juice
1 cup sugar
6 egg whites
2 teaspoons vanilla

serves 12

Lightly grease a 10 cup mold with oil or butter for easy unmolding. In a sauce pan simmer prunes in a cup of water. After they are soft, remove prunes and put in food processor. Slowly add gelatin to the lukewarm prune water in the sauce pan. Add lime juice and 1/3 cup sugar and heat, mixing constantly until gelatin and sugar dissolve. Set aside.

Process prunes with 1/3 cup of sugar in food processor until chopped fine. Add liquid and blend well. Pour mixture in a big mixing bowl, reserve.

Beat egg whites to soft peaks. Slowly add 1/3 cup sugar and continue beating until firm peaks form. Be careful not to overbeat. Fold egg whites carefully into prune mixture and add vanilla extract. Blend well. Pour mousse into prepared mold and chill for 3 hours or overnight. Serve unmolded on a platter with Quick Custard Cream on the side.

QUICK CUSTARD CREAM

2 cups milk
4 egg yolks
2 tablespoons cornstarch
1 1/2 teaspoons vanilla extract
3 to 4 tablespoons sugar

In a sauce pan combine milk, egg yolks and cornstarch. Heat on medium heat and whisk until mixture starts thickening. Remove from heat when first bubbles appear. Add sugar and vanilla extract and mix well until sugar melts. Pour sauce in a glass container, cover and chill.

Ariana Kumpis
Ariana's Cooking School
Member of the International Association of Culinary Professionals
Miami, Florida

RHUBARB SAUCE & RHUBARB ICE

Delicious with your favorite warm strudel recipe or over strawberry pie.

RHUBARB SAUCE

1 pound rhubarb, diced
1 cup sugar
1 cup water
pinch of cinnamon
pinch of salt
1 tablespoon fresh lemon juice
red food coloring (optional)

Combine all ingredients except lemon juice in a sauce pan, bring to a boil and cook over medium heat for approximately 15 minutes, or until rhubarb mixture is syrupy. Adjust coloring, if necessary, and add lemon juice to taste, amount of both depends on natural color of rhubarb and degree of sweetness desired. Puree in blender and cool to room temperature. Chill.

RHUBARB ICE

2 pounds rhubarb, diced
1 cup sugar
1 cup water
pinch of cinnamon
1 egg white
4 tablespoons cognac
1 cup dry champagne
red food coloring (optional)

Place rhubarb, sugar and water in sauce pan and cook over medium heat for about 15 minutes. Remove cooked rhubarb from sauce pan and reserve. Add a pinch of cinnamon and food coloring to rhubarb liquid if desired. Reduce liquid to 1½ cups. Puree reserved rhubarb with reduced syrup in blender. Add egg white and blend again. Blend in cognac and chill. Once chilled, blend in champagne, then freeze in rotating ice cream maker.

CAROLYN BUSTER
The Cottage restaurant
Member of the International Association of Culinary Professionals
Calumet City, Illinois

STRAWBERRY RHUBARB BETTY

Ron loved the blend of strawberries with rhubarb. This is a different version of an old favorite - a superb ending to a summer meal. Serve alone or with whipped cream laced with Grand Marnier.

STRAWBERRY RHUBARB

1 pint strawberries, halved
3 cups fresh rhubarb, cut into 1/2 inch pieces
grated rind of orange
1 1/2 tablespoons fresh orange juice
1 1/2 tablespoons Grand Marnier
1 cup sugar
4 1/2 tablespoons flour
1/8 teaspoon salt

serves 6-8

Mix strawberries, rhubarb, rind, orange juice and Grand Marnier together in large bowl. Mix sugar, flour and salt together in another bowl and stir well. Pour sugar mixture over fruit, toss gently, and fold together until fruit is evenly covered. Pour into a 2 quart round buttered casserole.

BETTY

1 cup sifted flour
1 cup sugar
1/2 cup unsalted butter
1 cup heavy cream

Preheat oven to 375 degrees.

Sift flour and sugar together in a bowl. Use pastry blender or food processor to blend butter into flour mixture. Blend heavy cream into mixture with a spoon. Spoon over the Strawberry Rhubarb.

Bake for 45 minutes with a drip pan placed beneath. Serve at room temperature.

GORDON AND CAROLE SEGAL
Crate and Barrel
Northbrook, Illinois

ACKNOWLEDGEMENTS

We would like to express our thanks to all of the people who helped make this cookbook possible.

ADVISORS

David Burkett
Polly Gaul
Patricia Levey
Katherine S. Reising
Cookbook Resource USA
Milwaukee, WI

SPECIAL THANKS

Jeff Cooley
Gail Christie
David Davis
Industrial Printing Company
Toledo, Ohio
Phil Margolis

PHOTOGRAPHY PROPS

Bill Alpert, J. Charles Alpert
San Francisco, CA
Bruce Andreozzi
Necessities
Brooklyn Heights, NY
Paula Brown
Frederick Cohn
Images Gallery
Kay Foster
Susan Gravely
Vietri Inc.
Hillsborough, NC
Shelly Julius
Rosemary Kahle
Julie Kiechel
Patricia Levey
Paul Angelo LoGiudice
JoAnn Kirchmaier
Phylis Mandle
Eleanor Menton
Eleanor McCreery
Barbara McKelvy
Adelaide Morris
Camela Nitschke
Diane Putnam
Glendale Florist
Betty Rank
Susan Reams
Kay Root
Patricia Secor
Francis Stranahan
Virginia Stranahan
Polly Webb
Georgia Welles
Matthew Weston
Matthew's Restaurant
Mary Wolfe
SJ's Emporium
Syd and Diane's Restaurant

RECIPE CONTRIBUTORS

Vania Alm
Dave Alm & Co.
Denver, CO

Madelyn Alvarez/
Dinah Vince
Gourmet Grande, Inc.
Cleveland, OH

Bonnie Aronson
J. Aronson, Ltd.
New Orleans, LA

Kay Ball
Perrysburg, OH

Scott Barnett
The Connection
Charlotte, NC

Priscilla L. Boelter
The Boelter Companies,
Kitchen Galerie
Milwaukee, WI

Betty Boote
HOUSE BEAUTIFUL
New York, NY

Holly Wynn Borden
Koehler-Borden, Inc.
North Canton, OH

Karen C. Brown
Kitchen Wavelengths
Toledo, OH

Carolyn Buster
The Cottage
Calumet City, IL

Hugh Carpenter
Chopstix
Los Angeles, CA

Carol Cole Caldwell
Food Consultant
New York, NY

Cheryl Chandler
Burdine's
Miami, FL

Monsieur Marc Chevillot
Hôtel de la Poste
Beaune, France

George Collins, Karen Dodge,
Jim Stirratt
Dayton's, Marshall Field's,
Hudson's
Minneapolis, MN

Wendy Condon
Walter Davis, Inc.
Dallas, TX

Art Conway
Young/Conway Publishing
Chicago, IL

Dominique Crevoisier
Les Halles
Montreal, Quebec

Glenn Cunningham
Lechmere
Boston, MA

Linda Zey Davis
Food Instructor
Kansas City, MO

Phyllis L. Davis
Walter Davis, Inc.
Dallas, TX

Jan Deckard
Rolling Pin
Jacksonville, FL

Jerry DiVecchio
SUNSET
Menlo Park, CA

Toni C. Douglas
The Broadway Southern
California
Los Angeles, CA

Elizabeth Duffey
Commercial Aluminum
Toledo, OH

Barbara Dunn
Village Kitchen Shoppe
Glendora, CA

Frances Enslein
Frances Enslein Cooking
School
Greenwich, CT

Judith Ets-Hokin
Judith Ets-Hokin Culinary
Company
San Francisco, CA

George Faison
D'Artagnan, Inc.
Jersey City, NJ

Betty Feeney
Betty Feeney's Ltd.
Boise, ID

Barbara Pool Fenzl
Les Gourmettes Cooking
School
Phoenix, AZ

Terry G. Fewell
That Cook 'N' Coffee Place
West Dundee, IL

Paula Finkle
Zachman & Associates
Miami, FL

Charlie Flint
Culinary Institute of
America (student)
Hyde Park, NY

Joanne Fortune
The Eight Mice
Lafayette, IN

William J. Garry
BON APPETIT
Los Angeles, CA

Nancy Gilbert
Upstairs Broadmoor South
Colorado Springs, CO

Judy Glassberg
TAG
Chicago, IL

Joyce Goldstein
Square One
San Francisco, CA

Kim Gonsalves
Executive Chef Culinary
Shop
Honolulu, HI

Ellen Gordon
Brookline, MA

Ginny Gordon
Ginny Gordon Gifts & Gadgets
Beaufort, NC

recipe contributors, cont.

Lester Gribetz
Bloomingdale's
New York, NY

George Gruenwald
New Product Development Group
Rancho Santa Fe, CA

Arlene Harris
The Chef's Catalog
Northbrook, IL

Tammy Hartman
Perrysburg, OH

Susan Heine
Island Kitchen
Marco Island, FL

Keith & Diane Heiner
Rolling Pin
Plantation, FL

Alan Heller
Heller Designs
New York, NY

Ruth & Skitch Henderson
The Silo, Inc.
New Milford, CT

Rebecca Hetrick
Commerical Aluminum
Toledo, OH

Carey Hewitt
The Cupboard
Fort Collins, CO

Kirk M. Holdcroft
UniGlobe Millstream Travel
Toledo, OH

Velva Hovey
The Dry Sink
Highlands, NC

Gene Hovis
Macy's
New York, NY

Robert D. Jaffee
Amco Corporation
Chicago, IL

Philippe Jeanty
Domaine Chandon
Yountville, CA

Melissa Jones
Peel 'N Pare
Fort Myers, FL

Sarah and Rosemary Kahle
Perrysburg, OH

Paul Kaplan
Bullock's
Los Angeles, CA

Becky Kasperzak
Perrysburg, OH

Laura Kasperzak
Roswell, GA

R. Michael Kasperzak, Jr.
Mountain View, CA

Sara Jane Kasperzak
Commercial Aluminum
Toledo, OH

Yoshi Katsumura
Yoshi's Cafe
Chicago, IL

Julie Kiechel
Perrysburg, OH

Elizabeth Timberlake Knight
The Cook Store of Mountain Brook, Inc.
Birmingham, AL

David Kobos
The Kobos Company
Portland, OR

Carole Kotkin
Food Consultant
Miami, FL

Ariana Kumpis
The Cookshop
Ariana's Cooking School
Miami, FL

Paul Angelo LoGiudice
Commercial Aluminum
Toledo, OH

Jim & Paige Lowman
Unpressured Cooker
Sanibel Island, FL

Denise Madden
The Kellen Company
Mount Kisco, NY

Roger Mandle
National Gallery of Art
Washington, DC

Bruce Marder
West Beach Cafe
Venice, CA

Phil Margolis
The Kellen Company
Mount Kisco, NY

Marilyn Maslow
Dallas, PA

Donna Mathre
Donna Mathre Gifts
Northfield, MN

Michael McCarty
Michael's
Santa Monica, CA

Mary Jean McDaniel
Walter Davis, Inc.
Dallas, TX

Barbara McKay
WBTV Creative Services
Charlotte, NC

Doug McNatton
Barbara Boyle & Associates
Los Angeles, CA

Diane Miller
Commercial Aluminum
Toledo, OH

Nan Miller
Perrysburg, OH

Laurence Mindel
Il Fornaio America Corp.
San Francisco, CA

Michelle Mitchell
Compleat Gourmet & Gifts
Littleton, CO

Margrit & Bob Mondavi
Robert Mondavi Winery
Oakville, CA

Jane Montant
GOURMET
New York, NY

Bennett Mulé
Onwentsia Club
Lake Forest, IL

Sally Jo Mullen
Les Chefs D'Aspen
Aspen, CO

Mrs. Richard Muzzy
Perrysburg, OH

Roselee C. Nichols
Palmer Island
Old Greenwich, CT

Anne & Bob Oswald
South Bend Escan
Indianapolis, IN

Ruthann Panowicz
Drees
Olympia, WA

Toula Patsalis
Kitchen Glamor
Detroit, MI

Jacques Pepin
Jacques Pepin, Inc.
Madison, CT

Sonia R. Perez
The Kitchen Shop, Inc.
Miami Lakes, FL

Anne Perry
The Cook's Shop
Somerset, United Kingdom

Clifford Pleau
Le Ciel Bleu
Chicago, IL

Peg Poling
Duck Soup
Ottumwa, IA

Wolfgang Puck
Spago California Cuisine
West Hollywood, CA

Gene Quint
Sign of the Bear
Sonoma, CA

Susan R. Reams
Perrysburg, OH

Lois Ringelheim
Fairfield, CT

Diane Rogers
Syd & Diane's
Perrysburg, OH

Betty Rosbottom
La Belle Pomme Cooking School at Lazarus
Columbus, OH

Jerry Rowlette
Rowlette & Associates
Long Lake, MN

Sally Hobbib Rumman
Sally Hobbib Rumman & Co.
Sylvania, OH

Carolyn Salas
Kitchen Stuff
Lufkin, TX

Jim Salveson
Los Angeles, CA

Cary Saurage
Community Kitchens
Baton Rouge, LA

Suzanne Schroeder
Spiaggia
Chicago, IL

Gordon and Carole Segal
Crate and Barrel
Northbrook, IL

Piero Selvaggio
Valentino
Santa Monica, CA

Glen T. Senk
Williams-Sonoma
San Francisco, CA

Bev and John Shaffer
What's Cooking? Inc.
Akron, OH

recipe contributors, cont.

Tom Shenk
Kellen Company
Annandale, VA

Sue Sims
The Pan-Tree
San Angelo, TX

Gordon A. Sinclair
Gordon's
Chicago, IL

Marion Smith
Chef Classics
Cleveland, OH

Jeff and Paula Solinger
Solinger & Associates
Clarendon Hills, IL

Pat Stanley
Aropi, Inc.
Atlanta, GA

Diana Sturgis
FOOD & WINE
New York, NY

Dick Sutton
Casey's
Williamsburg, VA

Irene Swaney
Jakarata, Indonesia

Fran Lucie Tallarico
Keokuk, IA

Judith Thompson
Thompson's Office Supply & Gifts, Inc.
El Reno, OK

Poppy Tooker
Walter Davis, Inc.
New Orleans, LA

Charlie Trotter
Charlie Trotter's
Chicago, IL

Leandra Walker
Gourmet Galley
Paducah, KY

Laurie J. Ward
The Village Gourmet
Evergreen, CO

Donna Warner
METROPOLITAN HOME
New York, NY

George Watts
Watts Tea Shop
Milwaukee, WI

Polly Webb
Toledo, OH

Evelyn Weeks
The Kitchenry
Lake Charles, LA

Georgia Welles
Perrysburg, OH

Matthew Weston
Matthew's Creative Cuisine
Toledo, OH

Madelin & David Wexler
Cahners Publishing Co.
Des Plaines, IL

Chuck Williams
Williams-Sonoma
San Francisco, CA

Geneva Williams
Gourmet Curiosities, Etc.
Sylvania, OH

Carolyn Yorston
La Jolla, CA

Brother H. Zaccarelli
California Culinary Academy
San Francisco, CA

Kristen Zachman
Zachman & Associates
Sanibel, FL

Yuval Zaliouk
YZ Enterprises, Inc.
Maumee, OH

RECIPE TESTERS

Gerry Ashley
Ann Broderick
Paula Brown
Dan Brumenshenkel
Kathleen Connell
Patrick Dittoe
Elizabeth Duffey
Kay Foster
Julie Gifford
Rebecca Hetrick
John Julius
Shelly Julius
Becky Kasperzak
Betsy Kelsy
Kathy Lawrence
JoAnn Kirchmaier
Ellie Menton
Barbara McKelvy
Carol Orser
Kay Root
Gingi Rothman
Julie Kiechel
Carol Sherry
Polly Webb
Matthew Weston

A

B

C

D

E

F

G

H

I

J

L

M

Q

R

S

T

U

V

W

Z